BECOME FIRE!

*Guideposts for
Interspiritual Pilgrims*

BECOME FIRE!

Guideposts for Interspiritual Pilgrims

BRUCE G. EPPERLY

BECOME FIRE!

Copyright © 2018 Bruce G. Epperly. Published by Anamchara Books, a Division of Harding House Publishing Service, Inc. All rights reserved. No part of this publication may be reproduced or transmitted in any form or by any means, electronic or mechanical, including photocopying, recording, taping, or any information storage and retrieval system, without permission from the publisher.

Anamchara Books
Vestal, NY 13850
www.anamcharabooks.com

9 8 7 6 5 4 3

IngramSpark 2020 paperback ISBN: 978-1-62524-788-9

Author: Bruce G. Epperly

Printed in the United States of America.

All scripture quotations are taken from the New Revised Standard Version Bible, copyright 1989, Division of Christian Education of the National Council of the Churches of Christ in the United States of America. Used by permission. All rights reserved. The author has made some minor changes to create more gender-inclusive language.

CONTENTS

Preface: Light on the Path	*7*
1. Becoming Fire: Adventurous Spirituality in a Pluralistic Age	*12*
2. Prayer in the Universe: Thanksgiving and Praise	*50*
3. Prayer and the Butterfly Effect: Intercession, Confession, Petition	*70*
4. Centering Prayer in a Global Perspective	*93*
5. Gospel Healing	*103*
6. Spirituality, Medicine, and Healing	*117*
7. The Energy of Love	*132*
8. The Power of Affirmative Spirituality	*145*
9. Contemplation and Action	*156*
10. Spirituality and Social Justice	*168*
11. Spirituality for All the Seasons of Life	*178*
12. Walking in Holiness and Wonder	*196*
13. Rejoicing in Multiplicity	*207*
14. The Blessing Way	*214*
References	*218*

PRELUDE
LIGHT ON THE PATH

How precious is your steadfast love, O God!
All people may take refuge in the shadow of your wings.
They feast on the abundance of your house,
and you give them drink from the river of your delights.
For with you is the fountain of life;
in your light we see light.

Psalm 36:7–6

God delights in diversity. Diversity characterizes the creative processes that give birth to a wondrous variety of belief systems, cultures, rituals, races, and personality types, not to mention the myriad genus, species, flora, and fauna that populate the Earth and the cosmos from which our planet emerged. The spiritual landscape is also dynamic, diverse, and evolving. Yes, God delights in diversity.

The wondrous diversity of spiritual paths is evident in the growing interest in global spirituality. Persons find spiritual illumination from a variety of wisdom traditions, creating a bricolage of spiritual practices from the many possibilities available to them. A friend of mine describes herself as a Buddhapalian, another as a Bapticostal, and still another calls himself a Bu-Jew. Each has embraced spiritual pathways that once were seen as incompatible, if not heretical, by earlier generations.

Take a spiritual journey back to the 1950s. Imagine a Buddhist being an active Episcopalian, a Baptist speaking in tongues, or a Reformed Jew going on Zen Buddhist retreats! Imagine a Methodist delighting in the poetry of the Muslim Rumi or a Roman Catholic finding wisdom in the Tao Te Ching, the primary text of Taoism, one of China's great spiritual traditions.

While some religious purists seek clear boundaries among the religious traditions, other seekers are discovering a creative and lively interspirituality that joins diverse religious traditions in a common quest for wholeness, justice, and enlightenment. Rather than seeking homogenous uniformity in doctrine and spirituality, spiritual pilgrims are delighting in diverse practices and theological nuances within their own faiths and the faiths they are exploring. Christians are joining East and West in creating new forms of Christianity, blending Eastern Orthodox and North American Protestant wisdom, while also embracing the insights of the East and Middle East embodied in Hinduism,

Buddhism, and Islam. The faith of others is seen as a blessing to deepen our spirits, not a threat to our beloved traditions. This is not a superficial "cafeteria" Christianity or spirituality, but a quest for wholeness and a longing to embrace human wisdom in all its wondrous diversity. It is a pilgrimage toward global citizenship in a time of planetary upheaval.

My own spiritual life is a microcosm of the spiritual journeys many have embarked upon in the last fifty years. This text emerged from my experience as a Christian who has found life and light in the creative synthesis of practical and theological wisdom from a variety of religious traditions. My spiritual adventures witness to the power of multiple spiritual practices and theological insights to give light on the pathway. Over forty years ago, as a college student, I learned Transcendental Meditation, and that Hindu-based contemplative practice inspired me to return to the Christian faith of my childhood. Today, I am a practicing Christian, committed theologian, and faithful pastor who believes that a lively, open-spirited, and spiritually fluid Christianity grows by embracing spiritual diversity in the quest to be faithful to Christ.

I am a theologian and minister by training, whose theological insights have emerged through my vocation as a spiritual guide and congregational pastor seeking to support the healing and transformation of persons and institutions, locally and globally. I believe that our faith is deepened and illumined by our commitment to finding God's presence in a variety of ways within and beyond our own faith traditions. God's revelations are intimate, diverse, dynamic, and varied, and—depending on our context, experience, and season of life—these varied visions and practices will nourish our spirits and inspire the next steps of our spiritual journeys. "The way, the truth, and the life," described by Jesus, has many pathways and possibilities for the adventurous Christian.

In the pages that follow, I will chart an emerging and evolving Christian spirituality for our pluralistic, postmodern religious age. As I embark on these reflections for global Christians, I am grateful to a number of companions on the way, beginning with my theological mentors: John Cobb, David Griffin, Bernard Loomer, Richard Keady, Shunsho Terakawa, and Marie Fox; and my fellow pilgrims on the global spiritual adventure: Jay McDaniel, Mirabai Starr, Philip Newell, Monica Coleman, Philip Clayton, Doug Pagitt, and Brian McLaren. I am grateful to Rev. Kathleen Kline Moore, Senior Pastor, First Christian Church, Falls Church, Virginia, who encouraged me to serve as Interim Senior Pastor for her congregation during her sabbatical; this text emerged from a Sunday morning study titled Christian Spirituality in a Pluralistic Age at First Christian, Falls Church. I have gathered further insights from my leadership of the Still Point Meditation group at South Congregational Church, United Church of Christ, in Centerville on Cape Cod, where I serve as Pastor and Teacher. I've appreciated the lively dialogue among the members of both of these seminars. As in the case of all my books, I am grateful for the insights and inspiration of my life partner, Kate Epperly, whose love for nearly forty years illumines my spiritual and professional adventures.

As you begin this journey in global spirituality, I invite you to open your heart to God's generous wisdom as it gives life and light to every path of healing and spiritual transformation.

ONE

BECOMING FIRE

Adventurous Spirituality in a Pluralistic Age

You are the light of the world.
A city built on a hill cannot be hid.
No one after lighting a lamp
puts it under the bushel basket,
but on a lampstand,
and it gives light to all in the house.
In the same way, let your light shine before others,
So that they may see your good works
and give glory to your parent in heaven.

Matthew 14:16

Be lights to yourselves.

Gautama the Buddha's Farewell Speech

THE ADVENTURE BEGINS

We live in adventurous times that cry out for bold spiritual adventurers. Christendom has died, and pluralism and postmodernism reign. Fires of the spirit are breaking out everywhere, and an emerging spiritual democracy has leveled the religious playing field throughout many places of the world. We can no longer claim to be citizens of "Christian nations," and, in many unexpected ways, this is good news. We are a gumbo of spiritual possibilities in which anyone with Internet or cable television can become a global spiritual pilgrim. Anyone who is spiritually literate, whether as a layperson, pastor, imam, roshi, or rabbi, has at least some general knowledge of the world's great religious traditions, along with a variety of emerging religious movements. Personally, in the spirit of the United Church of Christ affirmation, I believe that "God is still speaking," and that God's voice comes through the voices of Christians, seekers, spiritual-but-not-religious individuals, and people from the world's many faith traditions.

As we look at the realities of global climate change, economic uncertainty, terrorist threats, and a rising disparity between the rich and poor, not to mention the burdens faced by the middle class and unemployed, we are discovering that spiritual vitality demands that we seek common cause with persons of other faiths, as well as with those with no faith at all. Openness to the wisdom of other faiths challenges us to affirm and create vital and inclusive personal and communal visions and spiritual practices. As emergent Christian leader Brian

McLaren asserts, a strong Christian identity inspires us to commit ourselves to hospitality and partnership with other faith traditions.[1]

Philosopher Alfred North Whitehead noted that the most creative responses to environmental and social change involve initiating novelty that matches the environmental novelties we are experiencing. We may even choose to get ahead of the curve and create new social and spiritual visions and practices whose purpose is to shape the world in healthy and life-transforming ways. Openness to God's visions for the future challenges us to discover and promote new life where others see only death and decrepitude, and become partners in shaping the future of our beloved communities.

In the spirit of God's call to creative transformation, I invite you to join me on a holy adventure in spiritual growth, inspired by the evolving wisdom of Christianity and the world's great spiritual traditions, innovative global spiritual practices, and emerging and process-oriented visions of reality. I will explore the many resources of Christian spirituality in dialogue with the spiritual practices of the world's great wisdom traditions. Along the way, I will describe the gifts other spiritual paths contribute to the pathway of Jesus; at the same time, I'll use the lens of the spiritual practices Jesus has inspired throughout Christian history to examine these spiritual paths. I believe that all these practices are congruent with Christian wisdom and reflect the growing creative yet critical synthesis of Christianity and the religions of the world.

Like all other adventurers, we can't predict where the journey will lead. On the way, we will find ourselves traversing unfamiliar and exciting spiritual frontiers, guided by practices of prayer, meditation, healing, and dialogue. We will explore ancient and modern spiritual pathways and create new pathways of the spirit, and all of these will deepen our spirituality and challenge us to reach out to others with the light and love of an adventurous God. In the process, we will reform and transform our spiritual practices, visions of reality, and faith communities.

I write as a Christian, committed to the pathway of Jesus, whose teachings and way of life awaken me to pathways of healing and creative personal and planetary transformation. My commitment to Christ compels me to be open to ongoing personal and community growth as I embrace the diverse insights of spiritual wisdom givers, physicists, cosmologists, healing practitioners, and Earth keepers. Our task as spiritual seekers, within or outside our particular spiritual tradition, is to be companions in the healing of our communities and this good Earth. We need an illuminating and multifaceted spirituality to shed light and provide guidance for responding to the unique crises of our time.

BECOME FIRE!

A tale from the North African Desert Parents tells of an encounter between Abba Lot and Abba Joseph that illuminates our current spiritual adventures. One day Abba Lot went to see the venerable Abba Joseph to seek spiritual counsel. "Abba Joseph," he confessed, "as far as I can, I say my daily office, fast a little, pray and meditate, I live in peace, and as far as I can, I purify my thoughts. What else can I do?" In response, his elder companion stood and stretched his hands towards heaven. His fingers blazed like ten lamps of fire, and he responded, "Why not become fire?"

Become fire! Burn brightly, giving light and warmth to the world! Illumine your neighborhood and enlighten the world!

In the context of today's postmodern and pluralistic context, spiritual leaders, laypersons, and seekers alike need to become fire to claim their vocation as God's companions on an adventure in global transformation and healing. We need to experience the vital currents of divine energy, inspiration, and blessing in our professional, personal, and political lives. We need to become fiery—illuminating, warming, and guiding—in the quest to heal the Earth. Perhaps, we are already on fire, bearing within us the energy and wisdom of the birthing of the universe, and we don't yet know it! Jesus said, "You are the light of the world." Some five centuries earlier, Gautama the Buddha counseled, "Be lights unto yourselves." We need God's light—and experiencing divine light creates spiritual fire.

Diana Butler Bass and Phyllis Tickle have proclaimed with evangelistic fervor that we are in the midst of a time of unparalleled spiritual awakening and emergence. Within and beyond the church, ashram, temple, mosque, and other traditional institutions, a growing number of people are deeply interested in healing and spiritual growth.[2] Some have become alumni of their childhood religious traditions in their search for a global spirituality that embraces the best practices of each wisdom tradition. In the past few decades within the Christian tradition, spiritual leaders and congregations have held a massive garage sale, to use Tickle's language, letting go of irrelevant traditions, doctrines, and rituals. Freed from the weight of doctrines and rituals that are perceived as lifeless, many twenty-first-century seekers and spiritual leaders have gone on a spiritual shopping spree, reveling in the diverse possibilities for personal and community transformation. Many committed Christians as well as persons of other faiths have discovered a wealth of spiritual treasures right in their neighborhoods, not to mention on television and the Internet; and they yearn to connect these spiritual insights and practices with their daily lives and personal values.

Michael, an active Episcopalian layperson, begins each day with twenty minutes of silent mindfulness meditation, quietly focusing on his breath and noticing the stream of thoughts passing through his mind. A church-school teacher in her Boston United Methodist church, Cindy finds peace of mind through yoga and Tai Chi and attends yoga retreats along with spiritual life retreats at a local retreat center. Active in her Jewish congregation in New York City, Rachel gives Reiki healing-touch treatments at a local senior center and asserts that she feels greater calm and energy as a result of her commitment to sharing healing energy with others.

We are in a time of global spiritual transformation in which the boundaries of the world's religions are disappearing and hybrid spiritual pathways are emerging. Many moderate and progressive Christian congregations sponsor weekly courses in yoga, Tai Chi, Reiki healing touch, and qigong. In other Christian congregations, people are rediscovering the wealth of Christian practices, ranging from centering prayer and sung prayer to *lectio divina*, healing touch, and labyrinth walking. Spiritual teachers from non-Christian traditions such as Thich Nhat Hanh and Deepak Chopra write about the life-transforming wisdom of Jesus.[3]

These are truly interesting, enlivening, and often confusing times for spiritual seekers. Many persons practice multiple spiritual paths. They attend Sunday worship services, volunteer at soup kitchens, teach Sunday school classes, and regularly read the Bible. They may also look for guidance in books by the Dalai Lama, Thich Nhat Hanh, Deepak Chopra, and New-Age texts such as the *Secret* and *A Course in Miracles*. Some adventurers keep their spiritual practices in the closet, fearful that fellow congregants and spiritual leaders will critique or demean their "cafeteria style" approach to spirituality. Others practice diverse spiritualities without being able to join them in a coherent whole. Often Jewish and Christian congregations that sponsor yoga, Tai Chi, and meditation classes fail to connect the worldviews and values affirmed in these classes with the spiritual traditions of Judaism and Christianity, leaving seekers and congregants without a spiritual GPS to navigate the diversity of their inner and outer spiritual journeys.

I recall my surprise while listening to participants sharing their spiritual journeys in a course on new religious movements held at Wesley Theological Seminary in Washington, DC. Most of my students had benefited from participating in complementary medical modalities and multiple spiritual practices such as acupuncture, Reiki, Buddhist walking prayer, and Zen meditation, but none of them had shared their spiritual passions with their pastors or fellow congregants. Despite their obvious commitment to the way of Jesus and their mission to their congregations, they feared they might be judged as heretical or eccentric by their pastors or fellow church members. They kept their excitement and questions to themselves, following a spiritual version of the "don't ask, don't tell" policy and in the process began to feel a spiritual distancing from their local congregations and fellow worshippers. In the years since that class, I have encountered scores of Jewish, Hindu, Buddhist, New Age, and Pagan seekers who have synthesized various healing modalities, spiritual practices, and sacred texts, but who struggle to make sense of how these practices fit in with the practices of their primary religious traditions.

A good many mainstream Jewish and Christian spiritual leaders admit behind closed doors the importance of non-Western spiritual practices in promoting their own spiritual growth but they seldom talk about God's revelations outside of Christianity and Judaism. They too practice a "don't ask, don't tell" policy when it comes to sharing their personal spiritual practices and positive theological evaluations of other spiritual traditions. Seldom do you hear, even in progressive Christian communities, sermons that chart a sound theological pathway through the realities of spiritual pluralism, exploring with their communities a variety of dynamic and energetic visions of salvation. Despite the benefits they've received from their encounters with non-Christian or non-Jewish spiritual practices and texts, these spiritual leaders are worried that positively affirming non-Western spiritual practices opens the door to theological discussions they don't wish—or are theologically unprepared—to engage. Moreover, given the statistical reality of membership losses, they don't want to encourage multiple spiritual loyalties that might lead people away from their congregations. By default, many congregants assume that their pastors believe that only Christians can be saved, that Hindu and Buddhist meditation is destructive to our commitments to Jesus, and that religious pluralism puts our souls in jeopardy. Saying nothing says something: the silence of spiritual leaders creates a barrier against seekers' questions and the transformational practices of other faith traditions.

Though few mainstream—and virtually no progressive—Christians affirm a literal understanding of the scriptural shibboleth "no one comes to the Father but by me," their failure to creatively and honestly address religious pluralism in terms of theology and spiritual practices reinforces an implicit Christian exclusivism and turns many seekers away from the positive message of God's all-embracing love reflected in the life and teachings of Jesus. This omission shapes Christian attitudes toward the gifts of other faiths and the wider spiritual panoramas of our time.

Consider the following encounters I had with active Christians over a two-week period: first, a conversation with a small-town United Church of Christ pastor in which she shared her regular practices of Christian centering prayer, Hindu-based yoga, and Japanese-Buddhist-Christian Reiki, and then confessed her fear that if her congregants really knew where she received her spiritual energy, they might question her Christian faith and qualifications for spiritual leadership of the church. She confided, "I want to share what gives me energy and insight, but I'm worried that the church might consider my practices unorthodox and doubt my credentials as a Christian leader. The more rationalistic members of my church might think I'd gone off the deep end, practicing some form of woo-woo religion." A few days later, during a coffee break at a spiritual retreat I was leading, a lay leader from this same pastor's congregation lamented, "No one seems to be spiritual in our church. We're so old school and rationalistic that I'm not sure I could find anyone who would want to meditate or practice healing prayer if I offered a class. I'm not even sure that our pastor feels comfortable with spiritual matters. I love our church and its fellowship, but I need something more. I wonder if my pastor would judge me for my commitment to Buddhist walking prayer and Reiki healing touch."

I believe that my encounters with the pastor and layperson were synchronistic in the Jungian sense: they were coincidental and yet meaningful. At the time, I wondered what spiritual fires would be ignited in this struggling congregation if these two women shared the practices that gave them light and energy. Although I knew I could not break confidentiality and "out" the pastor to her congregant, I drove home filled with questions: Could there be other persons in the church and local community who are in search of deeper and more dynamic spiritual experiences? What would happen if the pastor preached about a diversity of divine revelations, broadcast in various ways among the world's religions and nonreligious seekers?

Unbeknownst to them at the time, the fires of the Spirit were illuminating a pathway for pastor and congregant to venture beyond their comfort zones. Inspired by our conversations, these two women eventually shared their spiritual journeys, first with each other and then with the wider community. In their creative excitement at finding themselves to be kindred spirits, they started a Christian meditation and healing group, utilizing a variety of global spiritual practices, including centering prayer, visualization, and Reiki healing touch. Their synergy has created a space for other spiritual adventurers and seekers, and has awakened the congregation as a whole to a mission that joins prayer and social concern.

ADVENTURES IN THEOSPIRITUALITY

I recently coined the word "theospirituality" to describe my vision of the unity of theology and spiritual practice in ways that transform our lives and inspire us to be God's partners in healing the world. Our beliefs and spiritual practices evolve in a lively spiritual synergy. Our vision of reality—our personal or communal theology—is lifeless apart from the concreteness of everyday spiritual experiences, and our spiritual experiences find guidance and gravitas as a result of vision-inspired theological reflection.

What we believe shapes our spiritual practices, and our practices enliven, energize, and embody our beliefs. Today we need to think big theologically and create pathways that join faith and action with the insights of the great wisdom traditions. We grow in spiritual stature by embracing rather than excluding. We need to nurture great thoughts and expansive experiences, and this comes from digging deep into our own tradition's spiritual resources as we also welcome the insights of other religious traditions.

This isn't a matter of personal preference but an affirmation of the interdependence of life and the universality of divine revelation. We are both one and many in the intricate interrelatedness of life, described by Buddhist teacher Thich Nhat Hanh as "interbeing." Our uniqueness flows out of our connectedness to the world around us—and then it creates a life-giving cycle that contributes to that interconnection. Moreover, in the context of religious pluralism and multiple spiritualities available to people today, we need more, rather than less, theological reflection that is both inspirational and insightful, in order to respond to the pervasive realities of relativism and consumerism.

We need to reach past deconstructive theologies that assert we cannot find any fluid and flexible meaning that goes beyond our personal or tribal experience. On its own, deconstructive thought cannot nurture minds, bodies, and spirits. Iconoclasm can be spiritually transformative, and we need to learn "how (not) to speak of God" and discover "the fidelity of betrayal," as Peter Rollins asserts; but healthy theological reflection and spiritual practice needs something more—tentative and lively visions of God and the world—to nourish our spirits and give guidance on the journey.

A SYNERGISTIC FAITH

I believe that persons of other faiths can learn from one another. A robust commitment to your own religious tradition can be the inspiration to seek wisdom locally and globally, while remembering that no image of the divine is ever complete. As a Christian, fidelity to Christ encourages me to commit myself to interfaith and interspiritual adventures. My understanding of the pathway of Jesus is illuminated by my encounters with the teachings of the Dalai Lama, Thich Nhat Hanh, Rumi, Abraham Joshua Heschel and Martin Buber, the Tao Te Ching, Sufis, Native American spirituality, Transcendental Meditation, and African Yoruba. Still, we need searchlights to guide our global spiritual journeys.

While the Bible does not explicitly address religious multiplicity, except in the case of conflicts between Jahweh, the God of Abraham, Isaac, and Jacob, and local Canaanite fertility gods, early Christians had a surprising tolerance for religious and cultural pluralism. Christian openness to the insights of the larger culture is reflected in the fact that Gentiles were welcomed into the Jesus movement without needing to practice the Mosaic law in its entirety; the New Testament is written in the Greek language and in places reflects Platonic philosophy rather than the Hebraic theological origins of the Jesus movement; and early Christian theologians, beginning with the Apostle Paul and the author of John's Gospel, utilized Greek philosophical concepts to express their understanding of God's activity in the world, the Incarnation, and the life of Jesus. Some of the earliest Christian theologians asserted that all truth is congruent with Christian truth, and wherever truth is experienced, regardless of culture or religion, God is its source. Certainly, the graceful vision of Christ, whose aim is to provide pathways to salvation for all creation even if it means personal sacrifice, finds embodiment in the Buddhist bodhisattva's vows to seek enlightenment for the liberation of all sentient beings, or as Buddhist teacher Pema Chodron asserts, "to wake up not just for himself [or herself] but for the welfare of all sentient beings."[4] Today, open-spirited Buddhists and Christians can affirm with Thich Nhat Hanh both the living Buddha and the living Christ.

As we look at the wonderful world of religious pluralism, we soon discover that interfaith and interspiritual dialogue emerges from a dynamic interplay of listening and sharing. We grow in wisdom and stature by listening to neighbors from other religious traditions share their beliefs and practices. We also gain stature by articulating our own beliefs and practices in ways that promote understanding and common ground. If God is omnipresent and seeks abundant life for all creation, then God is positively influencing everyone, regardless of religious tradition or culture. All persons, without exception, can experience God's guidance through synchronous encounters, insights, intuitions, dreams, communal worship, and mystical experiences.

God's witness is everywhere. The great religious teachers and founders of the world's spiritual movements were touched by God in ways that gave them insight and enlightenment and enabled them to share divine wisdom and blessing in their time and place. Surely, wherever truth and healing occur, God is present, even if God's name is not invoked. We are, as the German mystic Meister Eckhardt proclaimed, "words of God"; and divine wisdom speaks through companions from other faith traditions. We may grow by hearing a Hindu describe her experience of Jesus or a Buddhist talk about the influence of Mohammed on his spiritual journey. We may recover an appreciation for the holiness of the nonhuman world and the cycles of nature by interpreting Jesus's admonition to consider the lilies in prayerful dialogue with a creation-affirming Pagan or First Nations medicine person.

I believe that God wants every person to experience the fullness of life. God has provided life-giving spiritual pathways appropriate to every generation, culture, season of life, and personality type. I also believe that God wants us to dream big and ground our evolving dreams in the realities of everyday life. Jesus once told his followers that they will do greater things than he did in bringing God's good news to all creation (John 14:12–14). While Jesus didn't fill in the details of the great things that lie ahead for us, the open-endedness of his promise is an invitation to adventure, based on God's desire for us to experience the Holy as a living, breathing, transforming, and energizing reality in our own personal lives and in our encounters with the visionary experiences of spiritual pioneers from every age and continent. Spiritual frontiers always beckon us toward more than we can ask or imagine! God is adventurous and wants us to be adventurous, too!

AFFIRMATIONS FOR GLOBAL ADVENTURERS

Theological reflection—imaginative visioning of the ultimate realities of life—is intended to be adventurous. Visionary reflection never stands still but is kinetic and kaleidoscopic. What some people describe as the "old-time religion" was a novelty in its own time, often criticized for its innovative concepts and practices. A truly holistic vision of life challenges us to push forward the frontiers of belief and practice, looking for light and fire in unexpected places and discovering new energies through unexpected synergies.

For many people, theology is a rare and often fatal disease that afflicts PhDs and people who think too much for their own good. These folks are often surprised when I point back at them and say, "You're a theologian, too." Anyone who thinks about the ultimate realities of life, mortality, suffering, vocation, and what it means to live a good and useful life is a theologian. I believe that visionary thinking and lively spirituality fit together. What we believe shapes what we experience and how we interpret the events of our lives. What we experience, often as a result of our practices, shapes our understanding of the world. Transforming moments can turn our world upside down and give us a new perspective on our lives and the world, whether these occur on walking the road to Damascus, meditating under the Bodhi tree, seeking guidance in an Arabian cave, on our back porch watching fireflies on a summer evening, or posting on Facebook. Visionary theology is irrelevant if it never touches the ground, unaffected by economic issues, family life, war and peace, religious diversity, and politics. I'm sure this is what the mystic Etty Hellisum, who died during the Holocaust, meant when she spoke of our mission in terms of the quest to become "thinking hearts."

Spiritual experiences, both dramatic and undramatic, need visionary thinking, joining head and heart, as a way of discerning answers to questions such as: Was what I experienced really God speaking to me? Is my experience congruent with my community's traditions and spirituality and my previous experiences of the Holy? If not, should I reject my experiences or imagine the Holy in new ways that take me far beyond my previous comfort zones or the traditions of my faith community? Do my experiences enable me to respond more creatively and compassionately to issues of family life, planetary climate change, or economic justice?

Visionary theology is intimately connected with the ethical decisions and political involvement that shape our character and values. Only a holistic interplay of vision, promise, and practice can revitalize religious communities today, provide spiritual resources for seekers, and enable people to experience God in unexpected, transformative, and ethically inspiring ways.

In the course of this text, I will be presenting an innovative and dynamic VISION—a way of understanding God, ourselves, and the world in which we live. At the heart of this text is the visionary affirmation that we can experience holiness in our daily lives because the ultimate reality, which I describe by the word "God," is present in every moment and encounter. The affirmation that we can experience God in life-transforming ways points to three obscure, technical, but life-changing theological words. These words may seem old school, but I believe they are living words, filled with new possibilities for transforming our vision of reality and way of life.

Omnipresence: God is everywhere we are and everywhere we can imagine, without exception. Every moment bears witness to God's presence and activity. Every moment reflects a lively, loving, and personal energy in which we live and move and have our being (Acts 17:28). If God is everywhere, then we are all connected in and through God's presence in our lives. Our personalities are real and unique, but they unfold in a divine environment in which separation is an illusion. Interdependence, grounded in God's omnipresence, means that we are never alone or abandoned; our creativity and embodiment is real, and our lives emerge from relationships and shape future relationships. Our uniqueness is relational, not self-made. As the philosopher Alfred North Whitehead asserts, the whole universe conspires to create each moment of our experience. Our creativity is the gift of the ambient universe and its Spiritual Guide whose quest for beauty gives birth to every moment of existence.

Omniscience: God lovingly "knows" everything that happens in our lives and the world, without exception. God is both personal and transpersonal. God touches everything, and everything touches God. Transitory though we are, we are part of God's history, shaping God's experience and influencing God's creativity in life's dynamic call-and-response. Omniscience is unfolding, emerging, and evolving. The universe is unfinished, open-ended, and, to some degree, unpredictable. God truly experiences us, feeling our joy and pain, responding lovingly to whatever situations emerge in the unfolding of our lives. If God knows and is shaped in some ways by us, then our prayers truly make a difference to God and the world around us. God is always aiming at beauty, healing, justice, and love, and our prayers and actions influence and expand the shape and power of God's aim. Prayer creates a "field of force" that enables God's energy of love to be more lively in our lives and the lives of those for whom we pray. Omniscience is at the heart of Christian ethics and begs the questions: What kind of world will we give God by our thoughts and deeds, by our personal and institutional involvements? Will we bring greater beauty or ugliness to God's experience? Will we shut God out or invite God to be our companion in shaping the future?

Jesus's words, "As you have done unto the least of these who are my brothers and sisters, you have done unto me" (Matthew 25:40), present us with provocative possibilities that can shape our vision of reality and our ethical commitments. What if Jesus really meant that God is truly touched and transformed by our actions? What if we are responding to God, and shaping God, as we respond to others?

What if we are "cells" within the body of God, having personal integrity of our own, but also known and sustained by a holy energy that gives birth to universes, fireflies, osprey, sharks, and ourselves?

Omnipotence (or omni-activity): Perhaps, the word "omnipotence" needs to be retired for a few years so that when we next invoke this word, its use brings glory to God and hope to humankind, rather than fatalism and pain. At its best, omnipotence means that God has sufficient power and will to bring forth the best possible result in a universe of myriad actors, each of which has its own integrity and power. Our understanding of omnipotence, like all the other omni-words, needs to be interpreted through the lens of Jesus's mission statement: "I have come that they might have life and life in abundance" (John 10:10). I believe that we have freedom in relationship to God and that our freedom is always influenced by God's aim at abundant life for ourselves and the world. As the African American spiritual, born out of living with tragedy, proclaims, God "has the whole world in God's hands," insuring that despite all the devastating events of life, we will experience a "happy ending" in God's realm of Shalom (the peaceful, healthy, fulfilled way of life that is God's vision embodied on earth as it is in heaven). The affirmation, "in all things God works for good," means that God has the resources and patience to help us experience guidance and healing in every challenge. God provides a way when there is no way through the efforts of holy messengers and our own inspirations, which open doors to unexpected possibilities. God's power is found in new and imaginative possibilities and the energy to embody new life in death-filled situations.

KNOWING AND NOT KNOWING GOD

Our affirmations about God and ourselves give birth to lived theology and visionary reflection, which inspire us to explore the deeper meanings of our beliefs, recognizing that all spiritual conversation, doctrine, or God-talk exists in the dynamic tension of knowing and not knowing, the *kataphatic* and *apophatic* poles of describing the world in which we live.

Every moment can be an epiphany, an unveiling of the ultimate holiness of life, described by mystical affirmations:

Cleave the wood and I am there.

The whole earth is filled with God's glory.

The true light that enlightens everyone was coming into the world.

You are a word of God.

You are the light of the world.

Tat Tvam Asi. (Thou art That; you are the Reality of the Universe.)

This is the *kataphatic*, incarnation-appearing way, inspiring us to say with our Hindu brothers and sisters, "Namaste"—the divine in me greets the divine in you—to everyone, both human and nonhuman, we meet.

Conversely, energized by an infinite God, we can't claim to know with finality the ultimate realities within which we live and move and have our being. These negations of the *apophatic* way are ultimately affirmations of the mysterious wonder of all being, in which we can never fully know ourselves or another, much less God:

> *God is beyond all gods.*
> *Neti, neti; not this, not that.*
> *God is a dazzling darkness.*
> *You are a "thou," not an "it."*

A chant I learned at the Shalem Institute for Spiritual Formation, in Washington, DC, reflects the interdependence of knowing and not knowing:

> *Ageless and calm*
> *Deep mystery*
> *Ever more deeply*
> *Rooted in me (or Thee).*

The great adventure into knowing God begins with the caution that all rituals and words are finite. We must not, as Zen Buddhist teachers counsel, confuse the finger pointing to the moon with the moon itself. Still, even the most humble mystics are inspired to say something about their experiences of the Holy and paint pictures of the Divine, however tentative these may be. What we say about the Holy and how we say it can promote life or death, welcome or persecution, in a world of wondrous diversity and incorrigible otherness.

Just think about how we describe the relationship of God to the world. Power is at the heart of many peoples' images of God. They believe that every event reflects God's sovereign will, and, as Rick Warren, author of *The Purpose Driven Life*, asserts, God has chosen all the important events of our lives without our consent or consultation. A god who unilaterally chooses every important life event also determines which persons are chosen and discarded. This viewpoint implicitly affirms that lost and found, out and in, unsaved and saved, sick and healthy are built into the nature of things and reflect the deity's desires.

In contrast to images of divine power as unilateral and coercive, today's global spirituality sees God's power as all-loving and all-including. Our Loving Parent doesn't horde power or compete with humankind but seeks to increase our personal freedom and creativity in ways that complement the well-being of the whole, as well as our own individual well-being. God seeks abundant life for all of us. God respects our freedom but works within even our bad decisions to bring healing and illumination. God's love is reflected in both

Jesus's hospitality and Buddha's compassion, and in both the quest to have the mind of Christ and live as a bodhisattva, seeking the happiness and enlightenment of all sentient beings.

Others devalue the world by describing personal and historical existence as an illusion, suggesting that our goal in life is either personal enlightenment, detached from the prison of embodiment, or that this lifetime is merely the front porch to eternal life. They believe that social transformation is unimportant in light of the illusory nature of selfhood or the hope of eternal life. In contrast, today's global spirituality affirms the beauty of embodiment, community, and personal existence. When Gautama the Buddha counseled his followers to be lights unto themselves, he was affirming our personal responsibility in the quest for enlightenment, not denying the value of individual existence or communal relationships. The body of Christ (the Christian community) and *sangha* (the Buddhist community) both proclaim the interdependent nature of wholeness, enlightenment, and salvation. Mahatma Gandhi's integration of Hindu wisdom and Christian compassion also perceived Ultimate Reality as intimately concerned with the suffering of this world's outcasts and untouchables.

Still others see our lives as entirely foreordained either by God or the results of previous karma, accrued in past lives. Inexorable predestination and karma alike deter us from compassion that supports and transforms others' lives. When we believe that others' poverty or illness are fated by God or karma, we may believe these individuals are getting exactly what they deserve and that any positive interventions on our part are going against the grain of the universe.

Ironically, many persons who hold nondual understandings of reality and believe that separation is ultimately an illusion nevertheless assert individualistic maxims such as "you reap what you sow" or "you create your own reality." In an interdependent universe, it is more accurate to affirm *"we* reap what *we* sow" and *"we* create *our* own realities." Our relationships can cure or kill. Together we bring joy or sorrow to all living things. Our communities and institutions create heaven and hell right here on earth. Tragically, for children sold into slavery, refugees on our borderlands or in Lebanon and Iraq, or victims of genocide, there is no need to anticipate a hell worse than they are currently experiencing. To assume they or God chose these conditions is to close our hearts to the suffering of the world and accuse God of crimes that would lead to indictment and incarceration if performed by humans.

The ever-present, relational, and loving God I affirm is the source of wisdom and energy appropriate to every moment of our lives. God hears the cries of the poor and inspires us to act to alleviate suffering. God loves the world, embodiment, and personal uniqueness. God brings forth wondrous diversity and amazing beauty and seeks to save us from our own negativity and ignorance. As followers of Jesus, Krishna, and Amida the

Compassionate Buddha know, only grace can lead us to wholeness. We are saved by love and divine love provides possibilities for us to become partners in God's quest to heal the Earth.

Our vision of reality can be experienced. Visionary spirituality makes a PROMISE that ordinary persons as well as monks and mystics can experience God. You can encounter God in life-transforming ways right where you are in this very moment. Our world is filled with what the Celtic Christians and their Pagan companions describe as "thin places" that reveal divinity in a world of perpetual change. Every moment can become an epiphany, revealing God's vision for our lives and those around us. No one is excluded from God's inspiration and guidance; God touches children, aging adults, and everyone in between. You are a little Christ or bodhisattva in the making; in fact, you are already one right now! The realm of God is among us, and we are lights of the world, holy reflections of eternity, sparks of creation's first light, and eternal manifestations of the Godhead.

Global spirituality also provides PRACTICES that enable us to become fire and experience divine illumination in our daily lives. Spiritual practices are the heartbeat of this book. The ever-present God is often hidden by our frenetic activity and unfocused spirituality. Spiritual practices enable us to wake up to God's presence in our lives. God is in this place—and now we notice it! Grace abounds and revelation is everywhere; our desire to encounter God heightens God's presence and magnifies our ability to experience God. As Elizabeth Barrett Browning proclaimed:

> *Earth's crammed with heaven,*
> *And every common bush afire with God:*
> *But only he who sees, takes off his shoes.*
> *The rest sit round it and pluck blackberries.*

Practices enable us to live the words of Thomas's Gospel—"cleave the wood and I am there"—and then discover that "there" is everywhere. "There" is "here," right where we are in the messiness of politics, professional life, and parenting. You are "there," and so is everyone else in God's ever-evolving and ever-enlightening energy of love.

NEW HORIZONS FOR SPIRITUAL ADVENTURERS

Throughout history, people have fashioned varieties of spiritual practices to awaken them to the ambient holiness in which we all live and move and have our being. Grace abounds, insight is everywhere, enlightenment is the destiny of all—but we need to awaken from the dreams of distance, alienation, separation, and abandonment from God and our most authentic selves. We need to remember that if God is everywhere, we are always home and always in God's presence.

The story is told of a lively dialogue among a group of rabbis about the proper way to interpret Moses's encounter with God speaking through a burning bush. The question that most vexed them was, "Why was the bush burning but not consumed?" Around and around the conversation went and many interpretations emerged. Finally, one of the rabbis opined, "The bush was burning and not consumed so that one day as Moses passed by, he would finally notice it!" It's easy to imagine Moses passing by the bush, day after day, oblivious of luminescence and focused only on his commute to tend his father-in-law's flocks—until one day he heard a voice, felt the fire, and experienced the enlightening and liberating presence of God.

Bushes are burning everywhere. Inspiration is around every corner. The realm of God is right here and near each one of us. The omnipresence of God insures that each place is holy and each person divine. Spiritual practices enable us to experience the wonders of life, the beauties of nature, and the amazing realities of our own lives. The wondrous diversity of divine artistry invites us to open the doors of perception to experience the infinite wonder of life in a child's face, in the flight of monarch butterflies, and in the wisdom of the world's many faith traditions.

SPIRITUAL OPENINGS

I will conclude each chapter with an invitation to experience easy-to-learn global spiritual practices, inspired by the wisdom of the Christian tradition in dialogue with the great religious traditions. Our challenge is to make these practices as essential to our daily lives as our very next breath.

Spiritual practices are seldom difficult in and of themselves, but often persons give up on particular practices because they have trouble following them at first. They expect to be experts immediately. But practice makes better not perfect. Like any skilled activity, the only way we can experience excellence in prayer and meditation is by praying and meditating, and this takes time and commitment. Even baby steps in spiritual practice lead to great adventures in experiencing God's vision for our lives.

As we begin, we will experience four interdependent spiritual practices that will be foundational for the adventures ahead. They are rooted in the interplay of Christian wisdom and the global spirituality that inspires spiritual adventures among the many paths of faith, as well as the journeys of seekers from every perspective.

DEEP BREATHS FOR THE JOURNEY

We begin our adventures in faith for the whole person with the simplest yet most meaningful spiritual practice, the simple act of breathing. Breathing is something we can't live without. With each breath, we are inspired; we are inhaling the energy of creation, the breath of God moving over the waters, and Jesus's breathing in and through his disciples on Easter night.

Breath prayers are at the heart of my spiritual life. Before I begin my sermon each Sunday, I pause a moment to breathe deeply the inspiration of the Spirit. When I experience myself becoming stressed, I stop a moment to take a few centering breaths, reminding myself that I have all the time, energy, and resource to respond to today's challenges.

Take a moment right now to observe your breathing. Is it calm and steady? Is it shallow or rapid? Take a breath. How do you feel as you do what comes naturally, inhaling and exhaling? Take a few more moments for stillness. Do you feel greater calm and centeredness? Don't worry about random thoughts. Simply notice them and let them go as you experience the breath of God's creative energy.

Many people think spiritual practices are one more thing to do in an already busy schedule. Breath prayer reminds us that spiritual growth involves doing normal and necessary things in self-aware and focused ways. We can't avoid breathing. Breathing with consciousness, however, contributes to greater experiences of calm and centeredness. Our breathing can be a reminder in the busyness of life that God is with us, inspiring us every moment of the day. Breathing in the spirit of God changes our world even if our external activities remain the same. As Buddhist wisdom reminds us: "Before enlightenment, I chopped wood and carried water. After enlightenment, I chopped wood and carried water."

Two scriptures serve as the basis for breath prayer. Following his resurrection, Jesus comes to his disciples with a blessing:

> *Jesus said to them again, "Peace be with you. As the Father has sent me, so I send you." When he said this, he breathed on them and said, "Receive the Holy Spirit." (John 20:21–22)*

Take a breath right now. As you breathe, can you experience Jesus breathing in and through you? Can you experience the liveliness of God's energetic breath enlivening your cells and spirit?

The last words of the Psalms present a similar image of the life-transforming power of breath, but this time God's breath moves through nonhuman as well as human animals.

> *Let everything that breathes praise God! Praise God! (Psalm 150:6)*

Take a moment to reread these two verses from scripture. Now close your eyes, if you wish, and begin noticing the simple fact of breathing, inhaling and exhaling. Begin by exhaling any stress or burden. Take your time and breathe slowly and naturally. Imagine that each breath fills you with God's radiant energy of love. Imagine each breath as coming from God's Spirit, breathing through you and all creation, filling every cell of your body and every emotion and thought. If your mind wanders, thoughts intrude, or external sounds distract you, gently return to your breath without judgment or blame. After about five minutes, take a few moments to reflect on Mary Oliver's "A Summer Day." [5]

What will you do with your one unique, unexpected, and precious life, the only life you can live at this moment of time? Will you pass by burning bushes and revelatory moments because you have better things to do—or will you pause long enough to notice that God is present, in this moment, this place, this encounter? What will you do with the gifts of energy, breath, and insight that create a sense of life beyond mere existence? Will you experience God's breath moving through nonhumans as well as humans? These are the questions that energize and inspire the spiritual quest.

Each life and each moment is unique in its earthly brevity. Embedded in creation and joined with the experiences of the nonhuman realm through interdependence, evolution, and divine creativity, our lives are awesomely and wonderfully made (Psalm 139:14). Each morning is an opportunity to praise God and rejoice in the wonder of your being and all creation with the words of the psalmist, "This is the day that God has made and I will rejoice and be glad in it!" (Psalm 128:24).

BREATHING GOD'S SPIRIT

One of my wife Kate's spiritual teachers, Allan Armstrong Hunter, taught his students a simple breath prayer that augments what you have just learned.

I breathe the Spirit deeply in
And blow it gratefully out again.

As an open-ended prayer, you can substitute other words for "gratefully"—joyfully, creatively, anxiously—with the awareness that we can take all our feelings to God. The Divine Poet of the Universe receives everything we share and works with the materials of our lives to bring forth something of beauty. All you need to live and love and become fiery and passionate in the unfolding of your life's breath.

Another spiritual leader, Vietnamese Buddhist monk Thich Nhat Hanh, teaches the following breath prayer which has also shaped my spiritual journey:

Breathing in,
I feel calm.
Breathing out,
I smile.

When we bring our breathing to God, the simplest act can become holy. Every breath can become a prayer, connecting us with God and every living thing. You can experience the enlivening and illuminating power of breath when you are in a traffic jam, waiting in an airport for a delayed flight, or driving noisy children to a medical appointment.

AFFIRMATIVE SPIRITUALITY

Faith lives by its affirmations, which shape how we experience the many events of our lives. The use of affirmations can transform your attitudes and your behavior. The Apostle Paul reminded his Philippian listeners to "think about these things" (Philippians 4:4–9)—things that are edifying, sound, ethical, and healing of persons and the planet. Paul knew that our thoughts nurture our minds in the same way that food nurtures our bodies. We need soul food rather than fast food.

The spiritual practices of this text reflect the affirmative faith that has shaped my life. I use many of them on a daily basis or invoke them in times of uncertainty to open me to the deeper truths of life. These affirmations are grounded in global wisdom and the living impact of Jesus's ministry narrated in the New Testament.

Far from being abstract theological statements, these affirmations will change your life if you focus on them regularly throughout the day. You might choose one of these, or another affirmation of your own choosing, and live with it for seven days, regularly repeating it throughout the day or in challenging encounters. As Paul proclaims, "Be not conformed to this world, but be transformed by the renewing of your mind" (Romans 12:2).

God is present in all things.

God is present in my life.

I am a reflection of divine wisdom

We can experience God's presence in our lives. [I can experience God's presence in my life.]

Spiritual practices help us [me] awaken to and enhance God's presence and power in our life [my life].

This moment is a holy moment in which I am receiving God's guidance for my life.

I am a little Christ.

I am a bodhisattva [compassionate healer] in the making.

God is as near as my next breath.

Peace comes with every breath.

HOLY/WHOLLY READING

Divine word and wisdom flow through all things, bringing life and light to us moment by moment. We can find new inspiration in encountering ancient scriptures from our own or another tradition. We can hear God's voice in new and creative ways.

Take a moment to slowly and meditatively read the words from Romans 8:26–27: "Likewise the Spirit helps us in our weakness: for we do not know how to pray as we ought, but that very Spirit intercedes with sighs too deep for words. And, God, who searches the heart, knows what is the mind of the Spirit, because the Spirit intercedes for the saints according to the will of God."

Breathe deeply, opening to God's sighs too deep for words moving in and through your life. Listen for God's guidance in the silence. Experience God's Spirit breathing through your insight and inspiration. You might choose to ask God questions such as, "What is my calling or what are my callings at this moment of time? Where can I experience spiritual transformation?"

You might also simply listen to the word or images that well up from your unconscious, not randomly, but as a result of the interplay of your openness and divine intentionality. Let the word or image open you to new possibilities for personal transformation or discovery of your role in planetary healing.

What is it like to be connected with God with every breath?

You might also choose to read in a sacred manner these words from the Tao Te Ching, the holy book of Taoism, listening to the lively movements of the Tao, the Gentle Spirit of the Universe, inspiring your every thought.

> *The highest goodness resembles water.*
> *Water greatly benefits myriad things*

*without contention.
It stays in places that people dislike.
Therefore it is similar to the Tao,
Dwelling with the right location,
Feeling with great depth,
Giving with great kindness,
Speaking with great integrity,
Governing with great administration,
Handling with great capability,
Moving with great timing.
Because it does not contend,
It is therefore beyond reproach. (Chapter 8)*

There is always a deeper wisdom available to us in every moment of our lives. This is the healing and energizing wisdom of Jesus and the prophets, and it also courses through the practices and texts of faithful people in every time and place. Listen. Divine energy and insight are just a breath away. Become fire!

TWO

PRAYER IN THE UNIVERSE
Thanksgiving and Praise

Praise God! Praise God in sanctuaries and forests,
praise God as you gaze at the stars!
Praise God for mighty deeds of healing and liberation;
praise God for cosmic creativity!
Praise God with trumpet sound;
praise God with lute, harp, and synthesizer!
Praise God with tambourine and dance;
praise God with strings, guitars, flutes, and saxophones!
Praise God with clanging cymbals;
praise God with loud crashing cymbals!
Praise God! Let everything that breathes praise God!

adapted from Psalm 150

Behind her, it is blessed,
Before her, it is blessed,
Above her, it is blessed,
All around her, it is blessed,
Everywhere, it is blessed.

from the Navajo Blessing Way

A LIFE OF PRAYER

Prayer has always been part of my life. My mother blessed us with words of scripture whenever we left for school: "May God watch between thee and me while we are absent from one another. Amen" (Genesis 31:49). Our family prayed at every meal and before every car trip. My dad, the local Baptist pastor, prayed for the sick and dying and pronounced God's blessing on the congregants of our church in Salinas Valley, California.

As a kid, I couldn't even open the refrigerator door without an admonition to pray! My mother had affixed a magnet to the refrigerator that proclaimed, "Prayer changes things!" As a child, I prayed for everything from lost baseballs to sporting events and sick relatives. I saw God most of the time as a loving parent. I also grew up to believe that our prayers somehow influenced God and our own good or bad fortune. But nobody ever explained or addressed the tension I felt between our "asking, seeking, and knocking" and our "receiving, finding, and God's opening doors." We asked—indeed begged the Almighty—for what we needed, and yet we also believed that everything was in God's hands and might receive responses such as "yes," "no," or "later." We were told to go to the "Mercy Seat" with boldness; we were also told that God knew in advance what we needed and had determined in advance the outcome of our prayers. Still, we prayed—and still I pray—despite the fact that most of my prayers appeared—still appear—to be unanswered or deferred to a later date.

Today, I see prayer as part of a lively, interdependent, and wide-open universe in which there are no absolute guarantees but many provocative possibilities. I see prayer as a dynamic process of call-and-response, involving us, those persons and situations for which we pray, the world, and God. I believe that every moment of our lives God calls to us through possibilities, surprising and synchronous encounters, hunches and intuitions, dreams, moments of insight, and new perspectives on ordinary events. These mostly undramatic, though occasionally dramatic, revelations of God's presence invite us to go forward in living God's vision for ourselves and the world. I believe that despite the immensity of the universe and the comparative insignificance of our lives, and even our planet, our lives make a difference in the scope of things. Our lives matter and are important to God, the one to whom all hearts in every galaxy are open and all desires on every plane of existence are known. As the Jewish and Christian scriptures make clear, God needs partners in shaping history to reflect God's vision "on earth as it is in heaven."

Sometimes we call and we are certain God responds. We experience our cries and celebrations shaping God's relationship to us and the world. God's call awakens our call, sometimes out of need and despair, other times out of abundance and gratitude. However mysterious prayer may be, prayer connects us with God and each other in a synergy of spirit and flesh. My mother got it right—"prayer changes things!"

Meteorologists speak of the butterfly effect. A butterfly flapping its wings in California could theoretically initiate a process involving myriad small changes that lead to a storm on Cape Cod where I live. In a similar way, simple acts of prayer can set up a field of force that can change cells and souls. Our prayers can change the world, but more important, they can change us. When we pray, our attitudes toward one another are transformed, and our personal and communal vocations are clarified. As recent medical studies suggest, our intercessory prayers may be factors in promoting the health and well-being of those for whom we pray, suggesting, in the spirit of Bell's Theorem, that there is no distance in prayer. In a radically interdependent, intricately connected universe, two persons, like two quantum particles, are joined with one another whether they are holding hands, caressing each other, or visualizing each other's well-being from the distance of thousands of miles. As ancient traditions speculate, prayer may even break down the barrier between the living and dead.

While prayer is at the heart of Christian spirituality, it is also at the heart of human experience. Native Americans' sweat lodges offer periods of intense prayer. Tibetan prayer wheels efficiently enable prayers to radiate across the universe, even when we are performing other tasks. The Buddhist *nembutso* expresses gratitude to the Buddha for the pathway to enlightenment and places our lives in the hands of Amida Buddhist's mercy.[6] As a college student in the wild sixties, I danced with Hare Krishna devotees as we chanted hymns of devotion to the incarnation of the Hindu deity Vishnu. Prayer is universal in its quest to encounter the divine, receive blessings from the universe, and send a vibration of healing across the world. Prayer is the affirmation that we are never alone and that we are constantly connected with a cloud of benevolent witnesses and powers beyond ourselves that sustain and guide the universe and our own individual lives.

In the pages that follow, we will reflect on—and be challenged to experience—two aspects of prayer: gratitude and praise. Gratitude and praise connect us with God, reminding us of our dependence on God for every good gift as well as bringing to mind the interdependence of life, including the life of God, from which each fleeting moment arises. The practice of prayer is evidence of our faith that we are connected with an Energy of Love that has our best interests in mind.

All of our lives emerge from an intricate and dynamic process of cause-and-effect in which the whole universe, to greater or lesser degree, shapes each moment of experience. Acts of praise and words of thanksgiving proclaim the goodness of the universe and the Creative Wisdom from whom all blessings flow.

LIVING BY THANKSGIVING

The German mystic Meister Eckhardt once stated that "if the only prayer you make is thank you, that will be enough." The Apostle Paul connects joy with gratitude and his own sense of gratitude enables him to sing hymns in times of stress and danger:

Rejoice in God always; again I will say rejoice. Let your gentleness be known to everyone. God is near. Do not worry about anything but in prayer and supplication with thanksgiving let your requests be known to God. (Philippians 4:4–6)

Elsewhere, Paul sees gratitude as at the heart of our relationship with God and the circumambient universe.

Be filled with the Spirit as you sing psalms and hymns and spiritual songs among yourselves, singing and making melody to God in your hearts, giving thanks to God our Parent at all times and for everything in the name of our Lord Jesus Christ. (Ephesians 5:18b–20)

Thanksgiving connects us with the Source of every blessing and enables us to face life's challenges with hope and perspective. Gratitude is a practical affirmation of the dynamic interdependence that joins us with all creation in its celebration and suffering. Gratefulness enables us to experience God in all things and all things in God. It sees all life being nurtured by a gentle force that supports, guides, and heals without control, coercion, or domination.

In response to the interdependence of life, many Buddhists recite mealtime prayers. Before the meal, they affirm:

I take this meal in nourishment to all beings.

Following the meal, they affirm:

Thank you in deepest gratitude for sustaining my life.

One of the most famous Christian hymns of thanksgiving was penned during a time of mass devastation. Martin Rinkart, a Lutheran pastor in the city of Eilenburg, composed the words to "Now Thank We All Our God," during the violent upheaval caused by the Thirty Years War. Because of its protective walls, Eilenburg became a sanctuary for refugees. The close quarters created by thousands of refugees brought plague and pestilence to the city. Thousands died. When many of his colleagues fled, Rinkart was left to be the town's only pastor. Rinkart conducted as many as fifty funerals a week and over a thousand funerals in 1637, including his own wife's funeral. Still, Rinkart persisted in faithful ministry, buoyed up by his faith in God's providential care. Perhaps he was sustained by Protestant Reformer Martin Luther's insight that in the midst of life we are surrounded by death, but more important, in the midst of death we are surrounded by life. When we live by thanksgiving and connectedness to God, we are never alone but always surrounded by a cloud of witnesses enabling us to face tragedy and grief with hope and resolve. In the midst of ministering to tragedies almost beyond human endurance, Rinkart penned these words:

Now thank we all our God with hearts
and hands and voices;

Who wondrous things has done, in whom
this world rejoices.
Who, from our mother's womb, hath led us on our way,
With countless gifts of love, and still is ours today.

Thanksgiving is an all-season virtue. When we are thankful, our perspective on life is transformed. We see the wonders of life and discover hope in the midst of tragedy. We experience our lives as part of a larger tapestry of relationships in which nothing can separate us from the love of God. The guidance and energy we constantly receive, mostly in sighs too deep for words, dreams, inspirations, and synchronous encounters from our very first breaths in our parents' arms, will be our companions throughout life's journey and beyond the grave. God's care is not arbitrary but consistent and continuous: "Whether we live or die, we belong to God" (Romans 14:8).

PRACTICING THANKSGIVING

A life of gratitude is the foundation of joyful and generous living. Thanksgiving joins us with all creation in prayerful interdependence. We can experience the holy connections celebrated by sages and devotees of all religious traditions. This simple exercise awakens us to the Life that sustains us with every breath.

Begin by breathing deeply, experiencing a sense of connection with God's Spirit moving in and through all things.

With each breath, feel a growing connection with the good Earth, with friends, loved ones, and the many blessings on your way. Take time to visualize the good things in your life and the people who have made a difference along your journey. Visualize the Loving Energy from whom all blessings flow, moving through them and yourself. Bathed in divine energy, count the blessings you have received, graces undeserved but transforming and enlivening.

THANKSGIVING IN ACTION

Gratitude leads to a transformed lifestyle. In gratitude for this good Earth, we are challenged to be stewards of our blessings. Thanksgiving inspires care for the Earth and reverence for its manifold diversity. It also inspires appreciation for our human companions. The Christian scriptures counsel, "Pray without ceasing" (I Thessalonians 5:17). Ceaseless gratitude brings forth light in you and in all creation.

Take time to give thanks. Make it real. Don't just grunt at a checkout clerk, coworker, friend, or family member who has just helped you; take time to say, "Thank you." Don't be half-hearted or stingy in your gratitude; be generous and thank others at every opportunity—for a job well done, for their faithfulness, for breakfast, for good service, for picking up toys, for cleaning their rooms.

Remember people whose support and insight have changed your life for the better—mentors, teachers, par-

ents, friends, pastors, colleagues, spouses and partners, children. If they are still living, take time to send a note of gratitude, post something on Facebook, write an e-mail or text message, or make a phone call. If they are deceased, visualize them in God's loving arms and give God thanks for their lives, thanking them as well for their importance in your life. In the dynamic and open-ended communion of saints, those who live in God's everlasting life may very well experience and be enriched by our gratitude.

Just one word can transform any situation, moving us from annoyance to understanding, ingratitude to joyful appreciation.

Under your breath affirm your grateful connection with "The Spirit in me greets the Spirit in You" or the Hindu "Namaste," "The Divine in me greets the Divine in You."

Thanksgiving not only blesses the past. It opens the future, connecting us with possibilities and energies and giving us hope and courage in the awareness that we are never alone for God is near. One of my favorite sayings comes from Dag Hammarskjold, General Secretary of the United Nations, who was killed in a plane crash in Africa while on a fact-finding expedition.

For all that has been—thanks!
For all that shall be—yes!

The Hindu festival, Diwali, celebrated in November prior to the United States' Thanksgiving Day, affirms the victory of good over evil and the hope for prosperity and joy in the year ahead. In the spirit of grateful interdependence, take a few moments to breathe this prayer of thanksgiving adapted from one of the Hindu holy scriptures, the Vedas, remembering that God's light shines through the many prisms of human experience. Let God's energy of love flow in and through you with every breath:

> *Almighty One, if we offer you a devoted mind and heart, you will offer to us every blessing on Earth and in heaven. You give food to the body and peace to the soul. You look upon us with the love of a mother for her children. You created this beautiful Earth all around us. And in every plant and animal, every tree and bird, your spirit dwells. You have revealed yourself to me, infusing my soul with the knowledge that you are the source of all blessing. And so I sing your praises day and night. I who am feeble, glorify you who are powerful. I who am nothing, devote myself to you who are everything to me.*

Breathing these words, we open ourselves to the divine "yes" that joins past, present, and future in a loving creativity, constantly flowing in and through us.

PRAISE AND PROVIDENCE

Praise puts us in relationship with the Giver of all Good Gifts. Praise reminds us that we are not the center of the universe, but part of a multi-centered universe whose diversity emerges and is connected by one divine energy and wisdom. Psalm 8 gives voice to the wonder we experience before the God of all creation.

*O God, O Sovereign, how majestic is your name
in all the earth!...*

When I look at your heavens, the work of your fingers,

*What are human beings that you are mindful of them,
mortals that you care for them?...*

Yet you have made them a little lower than yourself,

*And crowned them with glory and honor.
(Psalm 8:1, 4–5)*

Radical amazement is one of the greatest of religious virtues, according to Rabbi Abraham Joshua Heschel. Praise reflects and evokes our amazement at the simple fact of living. It invites us to experience wonder everywhere and beauty in the smallest of things.

Pause a moment to meditate on the words of the hymn "For the Beauty of the Earth." Begin by taking a few deep breaths, centering yourself in God's grandeur and creativity in the world. Slowly read the words, meditating on each phrase, taking time to visualize the beauties being described.

For the beauty of the earth
For the glory of the skies,

For the love which from our birth
Over and around us lies:
God of all, to Thee we raise
This our joyful hymn of praise.
For the beauty of each hour
Of the day and of the night,
Hill and vale and tree and flow'r
Sun and Moon and stars of light....
For the joy of human love,
Brother, sister, parent, child,
Friends on earth and friends above.
For all gentle thoughts and mild,
God of all to Thee we raise
This our hymn of joyful praise.

Conclude this time of praise by imagining the wonder of the universe in the heavens above, the vast cosmic journey of nearly fourteen billion years and one hundred twenty-five billion galaxies (or more), and the reality that even this grandeur cannot encompass the Loving Spirit in whom we live and move and have our being.

For those whose praises are wholehearted, a new vision may emerge when we ponder the Earth in all its fullness and variety. The whole Earth is filled with God's glory. Accordingly, we don't need to leave the Earth to experience God's glory. If God is ever-present, then every place is home, every encounter an epiphany, and every moment a revelation. Heaven is right where you are: you don't have to wait till you die to see God face to face. In a God-filled world, the afterlife is not intrinsically better than this lifetime; it is just different, a holy dimension with no obstructions to our companionship with God and each other. This is the deeper meaning of the Hindu concept of the universe as *lila*, or the playful artistry of God. We can embrace the totality of life as both transitory and beautiful because the world was created by bliss, from bliss, and for bliss. Our joy comes from seeing God's wisdom moving energetically and artistically in all things, including our own brief but wonderful lives.

According to Islamic wisdom, praise can transform your life and free you from past sin. Reciting *"Subhan-Allah wa bihamdihi,"* which means, "Glory to Allah and praise Him," one hundred times a day will cleanse worshippers from iniquity and connect them with the All Merciful One.

In the spirit of praise, I will conclude these thoughts with two poems by Gerard Manley Hopkins, "God's Grandeur" and "Pied Beauty." These poems have special significance to me both personally and theologically. They were read by friend and fellow graduate student Catherine Keller (now a professor of Theology at Drew University Theological School) at the wedding of Katherine Gould and Bruce Epperly on January 13, 1979.

> *The world is charged with the grandeur of God.*
> *It will flame out, like shining from shook foil;*
> *It gathers to a greatness, like the ooze of oil*
> *Crushed. Why do men then now not reck his rod?*
> *Generations have trod, have trod, have trod;*
> *And all is seared with trade; bleared, smeared with toil;*
> *And wears man's smudge and shares man's smell: the soil*
> *Is bare now, nor can foot feel, being shod.*
> *And for all this, nature is never spent;*
> *There lives the dearest freshness deep down things;*
> *And though the last lights off the black West went*
> *Oh, morning, at the brown brink eastward, springs—*
> *Because the Holy Ghost over the bent*
> *World broods with warm breast and with ah! bright wings.*

And another poem from Hopkins:

> *Glory be to God for dappled things—*
> *For skies of couple-colour as a brinded cow;*

For rose-moles all in stipple upon trout that swim;
Fresh-firecoal chestnut-falls; finches wings;
Landscape plotted and pieced—
fold, fallow and plough;
All trades, their gear and tackle and trim.
All things counter, original, spare, strange;
Whatever is fickle, freckled (who knows how?)
With swift, slow; sweet, sour; adazzle, dim;
He fathers-forth whose beauty is past change:
Praise him.

Yes, praise God. Praise, praise, praise! Rejoice in the beauty of life. Walk in the spirit of the Navajo blessing, with beauty all around you. Give thanks on all occasions. Let your voice inspire vocation to treasure, nurture, protect, and grow this wondrous Earth and its creatures.

PRACTICING PRAISE

Contemporary seekers as well as progressive Christians don't say a lot about praise. Perhaps, this is because acts of praise are often understood hierarchically and dualistically rather than relationally and personally. Praise does not need to be understood in terms of a subservient relationship to a coercive, domineering, and distant masculine deity. Our understanding of praise can be transformed to embrace the vastness of life and the energy of love that moves through all things. Healthy praise connects us with the Giver of Life and the Giftedness in which we live, move, and have our being each moment and over a lifetime. Healthy praise takes us from duality to unity and polarization to community.

We practice praise by noticing the world in its grandeur. One way to experience the grandeur of life is to meditate on the "heavens above" as portrayed by the Hubble telescope,[7] view segments of Carl Sagan's PBS Series Cosmos[8] *NOVA's* Fabric of the Universe,[9] *or Neil de Grasse Tyson's update of Sagan's* Cosmos.[10] *You might also meditate on the wonders of the microcosmic world of our immune system. Perhaps, even simpler, is to wake up before sunrise and walk in your neighborhood, gazing heavenward. Even in metropolitan areas, you can glimpse the vastness that undergirds our earthly existence.*

I personally experience the grandeur that calls me to praise virtually every morning as I walk the circuit from my Cape Cod church past marshes, wetlands, and beaches to the Craigville Retreat Center and back again. In the quiet of the morning, as I open my heart, mind, and eyes in prayer, my senses awaken to God's voices whispering in winds and waves and God's moving images in flying osprey and glimmering waves.

When Isaiah encounters the Holy One in the Jerusalem Temple, he hears angelic beings chanting:

Holy! Holy! Holy! is the God of all creation.
Heaven and earth are filled with God's glory.

Glory can be experienced anywhere on heaven and earth. We can experience it in our one wild and precious life, gazing at a grasshopper, playing with a toddler, or meeting with a client. The universe in its wonder gives us gifts that are constantly "more than we can ask or imagine."
Praise God!

A BRIEF THEOLOGICAL INTERLUDE

Theology is about our vision of reality. Our vision of reality shapes how we perceive the universe and each moment of life. A world of praise celebrates God's original blessing of all creation. The goodness of life—every creature, plant, and animal—is primordial; our sinfulness and conflicts with each other are secondary. Although there is pain and death in the evolutionary process, and greater complexity of experience opens the door for the possibility of both more significant achievements of beauty and acts of destruction, a movement toward wholeness and beauty is at the heart of the creative process. Trappist monk Thomas Merton, a pioneer in global spirituality, described this gentle providence as a "hidden wholeness," undergirding each creature's existence. The Bible's first creation story (Genesis 1:1–2:4) pronounces the universe as a whole, including the heavens above, woodlands and plants, flying animals, sea creatures, and land creatures, as good.

Humankind is not an exception to the goodness of life. We are created in the image of a lively and complex God, embracing both male and female, and masculine and feminine, in God's relationship with the world. The philosopher Plato speaks of the universe as a shrine to Divine Wisdom and Artistry. The philosopher Alfred North Whitehead, whose insights permeate this text, asserts that the aim of the universe is toward the creation of beauty. Divine artistry brings forth cells and souls. The Poet of the Universe brings froth wholeness and beauty from the wreckage of our lives. The Navajo Blessing Way proclaims the beauty of all creation and affirms that "with beauty all around, I walk."

Healthy theology begins and ends with the affirmation: we are God's beloved and worthy children, *because of*—not *in spite of*—who we are. We are God's children, finite and imperfect, but made to experience and give birth to beauty and wonder. If we focus theologically on first things first, we will become natural mystics, ecstatically enjoying and cherishing the embodied joys of this good Earth.

SPIRITUAL OPENINGS

Throughout the day, awaken to beauty. Poet and theologian Patricia Adams Farmer invites us to embrace a beautiful God by awakening to the wonder of a sleeping cat, a cup of tea, a morsel of chocolate, and sunlight shimmering on the waves.[11] *Let your eyes roam the hallways, streets, and marketplaces. Awaken to beauty everywhere—in cars speeding by, the chirping of birds, the morning sunlight—giving thanks for the ability to notice the beauties of this good Earth.*

Live sensationally. Taste, see, hear, touch, and smell the goodness of God. Breathe deeply, eat with awareness and joy, feel the ground beneath your feet, enjoy your skin and the skin of your beloved companions. God's goodness is everywhere, and inspires us, above all, to give thanks and glory to God for this good Earth and all its creatures, bringing life and light to everyone you meet.

THREE

PRAYER AND THE BUTTERFLY EFFECT
Intercession, Confession, Petition

Eternal Spirit, Earth-maker, Pain-bearer, Life-giver,
Source of all that is and all that shall be,
Father and Mother of us all,
Loving God, in whom is heaven:
The hallowing of your name echoes through the universe!
The way of your justice be followed
by all the peoples of the world!
Your heavenly will be done by all created beings!
Your commonwealth of peace and freedom
sustain our hope and come on Earth.
With bread we need for today, feed us.
In the hurts we absorb from one another, forgive us.
In times of temptation, strengthen us.
From trials too great to endure, spare us.
From the grip of all that is evil, free us.
For you reign in the glory and power
that is love, now and forever. Amen.

The Prayer of Jesus,
A New Zealand Prayer Book, influenced by Maori,
indigenous New Zealand Polynesian spirituality

In the early 1960s, Edward Lorenz, a meteorologist studying weather predictions, made a minor an infinitesimal input change in his calculations. To his amazement, this small change made the difference between sunshine and storm in his predicted outcome. Initially, one of his colleagues asserted that if the theory was correct, "one flap of a seagull's wings would change the course of weather forever." Later Lorenz coined the more poetic term "butterfly effect" to describe how small changes can lead to great outcomes.

In many ways, the butterfly effect is at the heart of spiritual transformation. In an interdependent world, there are no small events or unimportant persons. An apparently chance encounter can lead to a life-changing experience. A forgotten word can be an agent of healing. What seems like an unimportant decision can change everything in your life.

Jesus's ministry can be described as the butterfly effect in action. Five loaves and two fish feed a multitude; a mustard seed grows into a great tree; a woman's generosity is remembered throughout the ages; and just a little faith can move mountains. Jesus invites us to ask, seek, and knock, knowing that even these small acts can open up unexpected avenues of blessing.

In the last chapter, we reflected on thanksgiving and praise as essential aspects of our spiritual adventures. Acts of praise and gratitude can transform your life and the world. Thanksgiving is the virtue of interdependence. Nothing is small or inconsequential to persons who recognize the interconnectedness of life and the impact of our lives on the world around us. Thanksgiving and praise inspire us to transformational ethics. They remind us that what we do matters to God and to others, and that our primary task is to nurture beauty and wholeness on this good Earth. Once again, take a moment to reflect on the words of Dag Hammarskjold:

> *For all that has been—thanks.*
> *For all that shall be—yes.*

Thanksgiving and praise inspire us to say "yes" to our human and nonhuman companions by promoting abundant life for individuals, communities, species, and the planet. Thanksgiving and praise enable us to say "yes" to the future, knowing that we are undergirded by the grace of interdependence whatever the future may bring.

The Kabalistic mystical tradition of Judaism proclaims that when you save one soul, you save the universe. The universe can never find wholeness until every lost sheep finds its way home. In the intricately connected world of the butterfly effect, the universe is not only saved one soul at a time, but one moment at a time. The momentary impact of apparently unimportant acts of prayer can make the difference between life and death for persons and communities. Our intercessions, petitions, and confessions shape the unfolding of the universe. Perhaps this is what Walter Wink meant when he asserted that "history belongs to the intercessors who believe the future into being." [12]

A-C-T-S OF TRANSFORMATION

Some people like to use the acronym A-C-T-S as a model for prayer: adoration, confession, thanksgiving, and supplication. Adoration is simply praise, expressing our joy and wonder at what God has done and is doing in our souls and cells, in the events of our lives, and in the broader world. Adoration is the great "yes"—or, as Anne Lamott puts it, the great "wow"—at all things bright and beautiful, all creatures great and small. Confession involves mindfulness and self-examination. In the practice of confession, we remember where we have missed the mark in our quest to embody God's vision of Shalom. We remember that our actions always make a difference—and sometimes for the worse, bringing greater suffering than health to ourselves and others. Thanksgiving involves affirming with gratitude the gifts of life and the wise generosity of the Giver of all good things. Supplication, intercession, and petition join our prayers for ourselves and others. In prayers of supplication, we bring our whole lives to God in prayer, seeking God's blessing and transformation of our lives and those for whom we pray. Small acts of prayer can lead to great changes in ourselves and the universe.

CONFESSION AND MINDFULNESS

Some people believe that prayers of confession lead to feelings of low self-esteem and unworthiness. They see confession as a dangerous act, centering on telling God and ourselves how bad we are. They rebel, as I do, at literal understandings of the words from the Roman

Catholic mass, taken from an encounter of Jesus with a Roman soldier. As he begs for Jesus to heal his servant, the soldier stammers, "Lord, I am not worthy, but just say the word and my servant will be healed" (Matthew 8:8). I suspect many congregants get no further than "Lord, I am not worthy" and fail to notice the joyful ending, "Just say the word and I will be healed." Critiques of traditional understandings of confession rightly note that most of us already feel unworthy in relationship with God, so we don't need to reinforce the notion that God loves us "in spite of who we are."

I take a different approach to guilt-ridden and shame-based prayers of confession. I see confession as an act of mindfulness in which we place our whole lives before God and come to know our gifts and challenges more clearly in the process of self-examination. Confession begins with the recognition that God loves us and wants us to be God's companions in healing the world. Seen from this perspective, confession opens us to an array of possibilities for healing and transformation. Confession involves our awareness of God's omniscience, that is, God's knowledge of us in our totality. The words "God knows" can be reassuring when we see God's knowledge as grounded in love and not judgment. God knows us, mirrors us, loves us, and provides guidance and possibility in light of who we are and what we may become in the joyful messiness of life. In acts of confession, we prayerfully discover that our thoughts and actions radiate beyond themselves, shaping our own and others' quality of life.

Christian scriptures proclaim, "God is love." Everything God does is shaped by love, including God's knowledge of us. When we confess the totality of our lives before God, in their grandeur and pettiness, we recognize that God loves us and is willing to help us begin again and again and again. Confession is not about our unworthiness due to some kind of spiritual disease, but God's unconditional love for us, simply because we are God's children. Nothing can separate us from the love of God, including our foolishness, finitude, and fear. In awakening us from our self-absorption, alienation, and apathy, confession helps us become transformed so that we can live in accordance with God's vision for our lives.

Confession is the appropriate partner to self-affirmation. A Jewish proverb states that we should always carry two messages, one in each pocket: the first says, "For me the universe was made," the second confesses, "I am dust." That's human life in its fullness, isn't it? We are creative, inventive, loving, compassionate, sacrificial, justice-seeking—and also mortal, limited, self-interested, and sometimes wrong and hurtful. But we are always beloved by God.

Surely this sentiment is at the heart of the Jewish High Holy Days or Days of Awe, encompassing Rosh Hashanah and Yom Kippur. During this time, we remember our sins, recognizing that they are part of the divine memory; we repent, receive forgiveness, and have a chance to begin again as God's partners in *tikkun olam*, healing the world.

As a child, growing up among Baptists, I often sang the hymn "Just as I Am." This hymn, like its popular companion "Amazing Grace," looks at the whole of life, describing the human condition as being tossed about by doubt, brokenness, pettiness, and alienation, but always able to come to God, welcomed as a beloved child, healed, and able to heal others through God's grace. We don't need to focus on the passages related to the blood atonement of Christ to recognize the realities of alienation and reconciliation that are at the heart of confession. Although God loves us in our brokenness, we may nevertheless feel ourselves controlled by forces that are beyond ourselves and stronger than our will or resolve. We may be the ones who build walls against God's love. Our busyness and self-interest may prevent us from hearing God's wisdom spoken through the still, small voice of conscience or counsel from a friend. Our consumerism may desensitize us to the cries of the poor. At such moments, the graceful energy of love breaks down the walls of separation, jolts dead spirits back to life, and restores hope to those who have lost their way.

Just as I am, without one plea,
But that Thy blood was shed for me,
And that Thou bidst me come to Thee,
O Lamb of God, I come, I come.
Just as I am, and waiting not
To rid my soul of one dark blot,

To Thee whose blood can cleanse each spot,
O Lamb of God, I come, I come.
Just as I am, though tossed about
With many a conflict, many a doubt,
Fightings and fears within, without,
O Lamb of God, I come, I come.
Just as I am, poor, wretched, blind;
Sight, riches, healing of the mind,
Yea, all I need in Thee to find,
O Lamb of God, I come, I come.
Just as I am, Thou wilt receive,
Wilt welcome, pardon, cleanse, relieve;
Because Thy promise I believe,
O Lamb of God, I come, I come.
Just as I am, Thy love unknown
Hath broken every barrier down;
Now to be Thine, yea, Thine alone,
O Lamb of God, I come, I come.

As a spiritual practice, I invite you to rewrite the words of "Just as I Am" to express your own spiritual vision and life experience. Where have you experienced separation from God and others? Where are you experiencing grace and healing? Where do you need to experience more healing and joy, to be in synch with God's vision for your life?

The following imaginative spiritual exercise may help you feel the interplay of wonder and alienation, and the grace that embraces us and all creation.

This is an exercise in Whole-Person Reading, or Lectio Divina. Listen to these words from Psalm 139:7–24, opening yourself to holy wisdom and insight. Take time to read them twice and then contemplatively listen for their meaning for your life today. Spend at least five minutes quietly praying or dialoging with the insights you discover in your encounter with the text.

Where can I go from your spirit?
Or where can I flee from your presence?
If I ascend to heaven, you are there;
If I make my bed in Sheol [the depths
of darkness] you are there.
If I take the wings of the morning
and settle at the farthest limits of the sea,
even there your hand shall lead me,
and your right hand shall hold me fast.
If I say, "Surely the darkness shall cover me,
and the light around me become night,"

even the darkness is not dark to you.
the night is as bright as the day,
for darkness is as light to you.
For it was you who formed my inward parts;
you knit me together in my mother's womb.
I praise you, for I am awesomely
and wonderfully made.
Wonderful are your works;
that I know very well.
My frame was not hidden from you,
when I was being made in secret,
intricately woven in the depths of the earth.
Your eyes beheld my unformed substance.
In your book were written
all the days that were formed for me,
when none of them as yet existed.
How weighty are your thoughts, O God!
How vast the sum of them!
I try to count them—they are more than the sand;
I come to the end—I am still with you....
O that you would kill the wicked, O God;
and that the bloodthirsty would depart from me—
those who speak of you maliciously,
and lift themselves against you for evil!

Do I not loathe those who rise up against you?
I hate them with a perfect hatred;
I count them my enemies.
Search me, O God, and know my heart;
test me and know my thoughts.
See if there is any wicked way in me,
And lead me in the way everlasting.

What images emerge as you meditate on these words? How might they shape spiritual practices and ethical behavior? What is your response to knowing that God knows the fullness of life, even the raw and vengeful aspects? What would it mean to place the totality of your life prayerfully in God's care?

Psalm 139 presents us with words of grandeur and violence, lofty thoughts and hateful ruminations. That's the nature of human experience, isn't it? But the key to the passage is the psalmist's openness to divine loving scrutiny and transformation: "Search me and know me." Confession is part of God's graceful healing process: we bring our whole selves to God, not just the parts we're proud of. We present God with failure and success. Confession places a searchlight on our insensitivity to the cries of the poor and the neglect of those we love; it also illuminates our feelings of unworthiness and low self-esteem, and it invites us to see ourselves as we truly are, imperfect but also beautiful, guilty but also beloved. This self-awareness becomes the basis for changing our attitudes and behavior, while all the time becoming more aware of God's love for us.

Remember God is not a hanging judge or gendarme, hiding behind a tree, ready to cite us for the smallest infraction. Nor is God a killjoy, eager to censor us for our sexuality or joyfulness. God is not out to get us or shame us, God's purpose is to love us and encourage us. From time to time, God's love may appear tough. The Divine Lover wants us to go beyond our comfort zones and launch out into the deep, and sometimes this may mean challenging us to dive in and then swim in the deep end of God's living waters. Our behaviors may place a wall between who we currently are and what we can become in God's vision of Shalom for us and all creation. Moreover, our apathy toward the impoverished and marginalized and our complacency with injustice may have hardened our hearts and deadened our senses to divine beauty and wonder. God may have to wake us up through challenging possibilities or unexpected encounters that reveal how far we have strayed from our calling as God's beloved children. Still, our distance and failure will not prevent God from loving us and presenting new possibilities and energies into our lives.

One form of confession or self-awareness is the Examen, a practice central to the Roman Catholic Ignatian or Jesuit spiritual tradition. In this practice, adapted for an ecumenical and interspiritual community, we place ourselves in God's presence, reviewing the day just spent. After a time of thanksgiving, we take time to remember the high and low points of the day, times we felt connected with God and our neighbors and times when we felt alienated or distant from God and others. We ask for forgiveness of God and others, and we commit ourselves more deeply to God and to self-awareness. The practice concludes with a short prayer asking to be open to God while we sleep and in the day ahead. Similar to the Examen, the Buddhist practice of mindfulness meditation (Vipassana) involves placing ourselves in a state of gentle grace, observing our thoughts and the day without judgment. In both cases, self-awareness is the pathway to healing and wholeness.

Confession awakens the spirit within us and calls us to action. We matter to God and to the world. One simple act on our part—like the flapping of a butterfly's wings—can be catalytic in God's quest for justice. One small turning—a moment of repentance—can change our lives, save a child, liberate a captive, or bring health to the ecosphere. Just as we are, we are remarkable and loved. Confession inspires the quest to heal the world one moment, act, and person at a time.

SUPPLICATION AND PETITION

In many Christian communities, the prayers of the people—a time of thanksgiving, intercession, and petition—focus on persons in need of healing and wholeness.

In one church I know, one of the members always asked for a community prayer: "I'm Fred and I need prayer." Fred's life had been difficult; he lost everything due to alcoholism, and now he didn't have the defenses and pride of the so-called self-made individuals. He knew he needed prayer. His vulnerability challenged the rest of us to take off our masks of self-sufficiency and recognize our own need for divine guidance, community affirmation, and personal encouragement. He was, as the old Baptist song proclaims, "standin' in the need of prayer," and he knew it. We may not know it, but each of us also needs the prayerful support of others.

Not my brother, nor my sister, but it's me, O Lord,
Standin' in the need of prayer;
Not my brother, nor my sister, but it's me, O Lord,
Standin' in the need of prayer.
It's me, it's me, O Lord
Standing in the need of prayer.
It's me, it's me, O Lord,
Standin' in the need of prayer.
Not the preacher, nor the deacon, but it's me, O Lord,
Standin' in the need of prayer;
Not the preacher, nor the deacon, but it's me, O Lord,
Standin, in the need of prayer.

It is right to bring your needs to God. Jesus once counseled his disciples to "ask, seek, and knock," and that applies to our own needs as well as the needs of others. When we seek, we find; when we ask, we discover answers; when we knock, doors open. The path ahead and the answers we receive may be wildly different from what we anticipated. But in the asking, seeking, and knocking, we may discover what we really need, clarify our values, and open ourselves to new divine guidance and energy. Our prayers, like the flapping of a butterfly's wings, create currents of grace that can transform our lives, heal our spirits, and contribute to the healing of the Earth.

When we pray for divine guidance, we receive pathways toward the future amid the maelstrom of our lives. Persons of all faiths can pray with the Hindu tradition the following life-changing petition:

Lead me from the untruth to the truth.

Lead me from darkness to light.

Lead me from death to immortality.[13]

Recently, at South Congregational Church, we created Christian prayer flags to hang in the churchyard as our witness to our commitment to prayer in the context of religious pluralism. Originally from the Tibetan Buddhist tradition, prayer flags reflect our deepest desires and are deepened and magnified as they are blown by the wind. Embodied in these flags, our prayers bless and bring healing to the world and ourselves.

They remind us that our prayers flow into the prayers of the universe, bringing joy to all sentient beings.

INTERCESSORY PRAYER

Medical research associates intercessory prayer with better health outcomes: when we pray for others, our prayers make a difference in their overall well-being. Although we cannot calculate their impact on others, our prayers may be the tipping point between life and death, success and failure. People of faith believe that prayer makes a difference.

I believe that prayer creates a field of positive energy around those for whom we pray, enabling them to experience greater health of mind, body, and spirit. Our prayers for others open the door to a greater influx of God's healing energy. Our prayers help God's vision become a reality in the world and in the lives of those for whom we pray.

Although our prayers are not all-powerful in achieving that for which we pray, many of us pray because—and not in spite of—the realities of pain and suffering. We believe that prayer makes a difference and opens the door to new possibilities even when the pathway to healing and wholeness remains obscure and uncertain.

PRACTICING INTERCESSION

Jesus says to pray boldly, asking, seeking, and knocking—and then leaving the outcome to God's wisdom and care.

Consider the following questions as you reflect on your own attitudes toward intercessory and petitionary prayer:

Do you ever pray for others?

Do you ever pray for your own needs?

What situations call you to prayer?

Do you think your prayers make a difference?

What bold prayer might you make today for yourself or another?

The scriptures say we should pray about everything. So take a moment, even with all the questions you may have, and pray boldly for yourself or another. In a time of quiet reflection, between you and God, take a moment for a deep breath, quietly centering yourself. What burden or possibility do you want to place in God's care? Now in the stillness, share your deepest needs and ask for God's blessing. You may choose to visualize placing these needs directly in God's hands, like a little child sharing a concern with a parent or grandparent. Visualize yourself as happy and healthy and fulfilling your most authentic visions and vocations.

Now place before God the deepest needs of another, asking for God's blessing on that person's life. You can visualize this individual healthy and happy, filled with God's healing and empowering light. Conclude by thanking God for blessings God is bestowing on you today and every day.

A THEOLOGICAL INTERLUDE

Our theological affirmations can transform our lives and shape the way we pray for others. Prayer involves blessing and not cursing. Ultimately, a life of prayer challenges us to pray for our enemies as well as our friends. Our beliefs shape our actions and can be a matter of life and death for us and others. When we pray, we are following the Apostle Paul's counsel to "work out our salvation with awe and excitement, enabling you to visualize and embody by your efforts God's vision of salvation" (Philippians 2:12–13, my paraphrase). Prayer increases, guides, and directs our energy and inspires us to seek the well-being of all creation and fulfill our vocations as God's companions in world-healing.

We can pray with boldness and courage because of the following theological affirmations:

> God knows us intimately and hears our prayers; our prayers touch God and invite God to transform our lives and the lives of those for whom we pray.

> God needs our prayers to bring God's vision to pass in our lives and world. They open the door for greater manifestations of divine energy and guidance.

> The future is open and our prayers contribute to shaping the future for ourselves, others, and God.

God's will for us and everyone is abundant life.

God is the source of good, not evil; God seeks healing, wholeness, and abundant life in every situation.

God balances our needs with the needs of others in responding to our prayers. God is able to intertwine answers to our prayers with answers to others' prayers, because we are all part of an interconnected web of life. What is truly good for you will be what is truly good for me.

While God always aims at healing and beauty, our prayers enable God to be more active in our lives and in the world.

A WORD ABOUT UNANSWERED PRAYER

This morning at a coffee house named Nirvana that I frequent near my home on Cape Cod, one of the regulars, an avid sports fan who knows I'm a minister, raised the question, "Why do athletes always praise God when their team wins? What don't athletes go public giving God the glory when their team loses?" He had a good point. In the aftermath of the Baltimore Ravens victory in the 2013 Super Bowl, Ray Lewis proclaimed, "If God be for us, who can be against us" as an explanation for his team's triumph. I wonder what the losing team felt about his identification of their loss with God's will!

I have always felt a bit ambivalent about such athletic witnesses. We need to expect answers to our prayers and also be humble whenever we invoke God as the source of our good fortune and the healing of others or when our prayers don't seem to be answered. There is no linear one-to-one correspondence between our prayers and positive outcomes for us and those for whom we pray. Our prayers and God's responses are part of a larger ecology, involving a variety of causal relationships. In reflecting theologically about the realities of answered and unanswered prayers, I have come to the following conclusions, all of them subject to revision, given my limitations and the grandeur of the universe and the mystery of God's creative process:

> We live in an intricately connected and complex universe in which we never fully know what's best for ourselves and others in light of the good of the whole.

> Some prayers that seem to be unanswered may be answered over the long haul rather than immediately.

> We aren't always ready for the answers we seek but must wait until we grow into the answers we seek.

> We live in a world in which events emerge from many causes. Our prayers are not omnipotent, but woven creatively through the events of our lives,

making a difference but shaping our lives and the world in light of our own and others' previous behaviors. For example, prayers for healing are woven together with a person's DNA, current physical condition, social environment, medical condition and care, attitudes, prayers for others, and God's vision.

While our prayers make a difference to God and open the door for more focused expressions of divine power, God also works within a multi-causal universe.

We may be the answer to our own prayers and the prayers of others. Prayer calls us to action, not passivity. We may need to act to bring about the changes we seek. God wants us to be partners in prayer, not passive observers awaiting rescue.

Although our prayers do not guarantee that reality conforms to our wishes, I believe that God seeks our well-being in light of the well-being of others. God's grace can transform our lives, overcoming the energy of the past, whether we describe this energy in terms of karma or family of origin. Still, the process of healing is always contextual and involves factors beyond our control, the most significant of which is our inherent mortality; everyone Jesus cured eventually died. The one prayer that is always answered in the synergy of divine call and human response is the prayer for whole-person spiritual healing. In the long haul, in this life or the next, all creation finds its wholeness in relationship with a living and loving God.

SPIRITUAL OPENINGS

A wise spiritual teacher once counseled, "Pray as you can, not as you can't." In this time of spiritual opening, simply pray. Let every event call you to prayerfulness. Your prayerful responses can be a blessing of a person on the street or a spoken or unspoken word of gratitude. It can be a cry for help or an expression of wonder and awe.

Psalm 46 invites us to "pause awhile" in awareness of God's care for things large and small. This pausing and opening to God can be lived out in the events of an ordinary day. This morning, as I walked the mile path from South Congregational Church to Covell's Beach on Cape Cod, I repeated the words of the psalmist: "This is the day that God has made, and I will rejoice and be glad in it." As I encountered the other early birds along my predawn way, I said an unspoken word of blessing on their day as I greeted them with a smile. As I felt a snowflake on my cheek, I gave thanks for the wonder of creation. My mind turned to my two grandchildren, and I prayed that they might be healthy and happy. I prayed for my wife Kate and a dear friend living with incurable cancer. I prayed for President Obama and the political leaders of our nation. I prayed that the President would find wisdom and that Congress would get beyond its gridlock and truly seek the greater good of the nation and world. I prayed for the day ahead—my writing, an upcoming prayer group, and an appointment with a congregant struggling with health issues, and I asked for wisdom and guidance in my pastoral leadership.

You will notice that my experience is anything but esoteric or dramatic. It is ordinary life lived out in mindfulness, seeking to pray without ceasing and encounter the events of the day with openness, love, and gratitude rather than fear or anxiety. My prayer echoes the vow of the Buddhist bodhisattva, who defers enlightenment to bring healing to broken humankind: "May all creatures be happy."

In the course of your day and the week ahead, explore the meaning of the Apostle Paul's counsel, "Pray without ceasing," by opening to God's presence throughout the day. Breathe a prayer as you awake, greet your partner or spouse, fix breakfast, pack lunches for school, greet a stranger or coworker, log onto e-mail or Facebook, and answer the phone. Your prayer can simply be a breath of love, a silent blessing, the Jesus Prayer ("Lord have mercy upon us"), or the Hindu mantra "Om."

Reflect at the end of each day and at the end of the week on the following questions: How did your life change as a result of seeking to pray continuously throughout the day? Do you notice new things? Do you respond differently to persons and events?

FOUR

CENTERING PRAYER IN A GLOBAL PERSPECTIVE

Be still, and know that I am God.

Psalm 46:10

Let everything that breathes praise God.

Psalm 150:6

We join spokes together in a wheel,
but it is the center hole
that makes the wagon move.
We shape clay into a pot,
but it is the emptiness inside
that holds whatever we want.
We hammer wood for a house,
but it is the inner space
that makes it livable.
We work with being,
but non-being is what we use.

Tao Te Ching, Chapter 10,
translated by Stephen Mitchell

TRANSFORMING MEDITATION

In this chapter, we're going to explore the quiet center, the still, small voice of God constantly whispering within us, around us, and through us in sighs too deep for words. Meditation has become an important spiritual practice among active churchgoers and seekers over the past fifty years. While Christians have always practiced forms of quiet prayer—for example, Quaker silence or monastic meditative prayer—interest in reclaiming and revising traditional Christian practices emerged in the past fifty years with the coming of Asian religions and popular methods of meditation such as Transcendental Meditation and Zen mindfulness meditation. Without disparaging other religious traditions' practices and belief systems, Christians have recently discovered a gold mine of untapped spirituality within their own tradition: centering prayer, walking prayer, *lectio divina*, imaginative prayers, chanting, breath prayer, and liturgical healing prayer. Many persons of faith practice multiple meditative techniques: Hindu Transcendental Meditation and Christian centering, Zen Buddhist mindfulness meditation, Hindu yoga, Hindu devotional chanting (kirtan), and Reiki healing touch.

By way of introduction to the practice of centering prayer, let me tell you my own story of spiritual transformation. My father was a small-town Baptist pastor in the Salinas Valley, California, and for most of my childhood, I was truly a child of the church. I played in the Sunday school classrooms, went on hospital visits with my Dad, and had my first paid job (25 cents a week) helping my dad do janitorial work around the church. (Emptying trash cans and unplugging toilets were considered part of a pastor's job description in small-town congregations in the 1950s!) I recall experiencing Jesus as a companion, walking beside me as I went to school in the morning and returned home in the afternoon. In the spirit of the hymn I learned in church, I took everything to God in prayer, including lost baseballs, Little League games, and family health conditions. I "came forward," as we Baptist's described saying "yes" to Jesus, at a revival meeting, "The Roundup for God," conducted by cowboy evangelist Leonard Eilers. With tears in my eyes, I accepted Jesus as my Lord and Savior and was baptized "all the way under," dying and rising with Christ, by immersion.

But, even as a child, I felt a spiritual void. I loved Jesus and felt his companionship, but I had trouble with what church people said about Jesus and his church. I heard that God loved everyone, *as long as they accepted Jesus as their savior*. If you had doubts and couldn't make the confession of faith, regardless of how good you were, your soul was in jeopardy. God stopped loving you and, worse yet, would punish you with eternal damnation. I discovered that despite our sinful nature, believers were the apple of God's eye. Meanwhile, dogs, cats, and dolphins were just window dressing, put here entirely for our use and valuable only as meals and entertainment at amusements parks and zoos. Although I had not yet met a Hindu or Buddhist, there was one Jewish family in town, and according to our church's doctrinal position, Jesus's own people were among the lost, condemned to burn in hell if they didn't turn their hearts to Jesus. To my father's credit, I never heard him preach about hell or the dismal fate of non-Christians; these harsh words came from other Christians in our church whose faith was a form of fire insurance, aimed at escaping hell and not bringing beauty to this good Earth.

My Baptist world fell apart when my family moved to San Jose, California, after my fifth-grade graduation. I was plunged into a world of ethnic and religious pluralism and, more disturbing, a neighborhood where church didn't matter to most of my friends and their parents. I had a crisis of faith. I didn't have words for the upheaval I experienced, but I felt as if the foundations of my childhood faith were crumbling. Was my pre-teen experience a spiritual emergency or a spiritual emergence? In any case, my spiritual landscape was shifting under my feet. I felt suffocated in worship services and often came home literally nauseated. A family systems psychologist might suggest that I was unconsciously bearing my parents' unspoken disappointment in God and the church after my father's dismissal from his small-town congregation. The unspoken stress at a world turned upside down from my father's loss of professional status and place in the social order of small-town America registered in my body. I believe, however, that something else was also at work. Perhaps, it was divine providence moving gently and unobtrusively through my personal chaos, luring me toward a larger vision of God and the spiritual adventure.

As a teen, I immersed myself in the sixties' spirit of the San Francisco Bay Area. I read Hesse, Tolkien, Heinlein, Emerson, Thoreau, and Whitman. I learned about Buddhism from Alan Watts and Jack Kerouac, and I discovered Hinduism, reading at the college library and discovering Steve Gaskin's lectures in Haight-Asbury. I imbibed in the psychedelic adventures of the late sixties and early seventies. My colorful visions took me far beyond the confines of my Baptist childhood. I discovered a wild and surprising spirituality in reading and experiencing the worlds of Carlos Castaneda and Aldous Huxley. I tripped out to the mystical invitations hidden within the Beatles' *Sergeant Pepper's Lonely Hearts Club Band*, *The Magical Mystery Tour*, and the *White Album*, as well as the mind-expanding lyrics of Jimi Hendrix, Jim Morrison, the Chambers Brothers, and the Grateful Dead. My "doors of perception" were opened wide as I experienced eternity in a grain of sand and infinity in waves beating on the rocky coastline of Big Sur.

Deep down, however, I came to realize that the fast-lane ecstasy of psychedelics was not deep enough to undergird my spiritual journey and would in time be my physical and spiritual undoing as it ultimately was for so many of my heroes—"Captain Trips" Jerry Garcia, Janis Joplin, Jimi Hendrix, and Jim Morrison. I longed for a spiritual practice to deepen what

I was experiencing through the use of psychedelics: I was searching for a living God in a faith, practice, and community.

On October 15, 1970, I found a path with a heart at the Students International Meditation Society ashram in Berkeley, California. It was, like my Baptist revival experience, the response to a spiritual altar call, albeit a very different spiritual call from the one I experienced as a child. It was the invitation to a transformed mind. I learned Transcendental Meditation as taught by Maharishi Mahesh Yogi, the teacher of the Beatles and the Beach Boys. I was illumined and enlightened. In one weekend, I chose to quit drinking, taking drugs, and eating meat. I did something just as bold—I returned to a Baptist church near San Jose State University, appropriately named Grace Baptist Church. There I found grace in the mentoring of John Akers, who saw a theologian hidden behind long hair and a scruffy beard. My encounter with Transcendental Meditation was the open door to experiencing Christ in new ways. I discovered the Bible again too, but this time, a Bible that spoke of care for the Earth and taught social justice. I also encountered a different kind of Jesus whose religion embraced rather than denied the wisdom of the Bay Area's religious pluralism. I found Christ to be cosmic and global, the companion of all, not just a few. Just a few Sanskrit words changed everything. A mantra opened the door to a new understanding of what it meant to be a follower of Jesus.

I owe a great debt to the wisdom of the Hindu spiritual tradition. I would not have recommitted myself to the Christian path without the impact of Transcendental Meditation (TM). The melodious TM mantra I learned in 1970 transformed my life. I gladly count myself among those Christians who practice multiple spiritualities: centering prayer and Transcendental Meditation, liturgical healing and Reiki healing touch, Christian affirmations and Buddhist walking prayers, Benedictine *lectio divina* and the simplicity of the Tao Te Ching. With the Apostle Paul, I claim with joy and gratitude my circuitous spiritual path to Christianity and the wisdom I still gain from encountering God in the wisdom and practices of other faith traditions.

COME AND FIND THE QUIET CENTER

Christian meditation—some call it centering prayer—is simply an extended time of focus on a word, phrase, or image as a way of encountering God, similar in approach to TM. As Herbert Benson's medical studies point out, meditative practices activate the "relaxation response," which heals us physically as well as spiritually. They calm our breath as we breathe in the breath of God. They heal our cells as they transform our souls, and they energize as they inspire our thoughts.

Centering prayer is simple to practice. First, find a personal prayer word—your spiritual PIN number—such as "love," "light," "Jesus," "Spirit," "joy," "healing," "wisdom"—and repeat it over and over again, moving from sound to silence. You may even choose to focus on words, or mantras, from another spiritual tradition such as "Om" or "Om Shanti," used by Hindus to contact the primal spiritual energy and unity of the universe. Whenever your mind wanders or you are distracted, you can bring your mind back to your prayer word without judgment.

The goal of centering prayer is twofold: first, to enjoy God in the holiness of the present moment, experiencing God's calming and sometimes challenging presence; and second, to gracefully experience the word and wisdom beyond the words as our deepest reality. God is present in sighs too deep for words in each one of us; as we enter the Quiet Center, we discover that we have all the insight, energy, and inspiration we need to serve God, love our neighbors, fulfill our vocations, and become God's partners in healing the world. Centering prayer reminds us that we can be still and know that God is present, that we can pray ceaselessly throughout the many activities that characterize everyday life.

God's Quiet Center is everywhere. From stillness come creativity and adventure. In moments of stillness, we discover the wisdom that gave birth to the great religious teachings. It is the gentle Spirit, the divine Tao, flowing in and through us, restoring, refreshing, and renewing. It is the hidden energy of chi, enlivening, energizing, and balancing us. It is the song of creation, whispering with the wind through Southwestern American landscapes, Navajo trails, Hebraic mountaintops, and aboriginal song-lines, that provides us with pathways through the wilderness. God is in all things, and in centering we discover the divine center in us, inspiring us to greet the world with the words, "The Spirit in me greets the Spirit in you." Namaste!

SPIRITUAL OPENINGS

Centering prayer is easy to learn and can be practiced anywhere. My favorite times and places are just before sunrise in my Arts-and-Crafts recliner chair, in the middle of a busy day, and as I take off on in an airplane. I typically spend about an hour a day in some form of centering meditation, whether practicing centering prayer (my prayer phrase is "God's light") or a mantra I learned from Transcendental Meditation. You don't have to go to an ashram to learn centering prayer, although I appreciate the opportunity to practice group centering prayer among friends, on retreat, or in a church school class, such as the "Still Point" at South Congregational Church on Cape Cod. The practice is simple and easy to learn.

Take a moment breathing slowly and deeply, inhaling and exhaling in a gentle rhythm. Feel God's presence filling your, body, mind, and spirit with every breath. Then ask God to be present, revealed in stillness as well as sound. Begin your focus on your prayer word, gently repeating it. When your mind wanders, bring yourself back to your prayer word without judgment. Even distractions can call you to prayer and, as some spiritual teachers assert, a cleansing of the unconscious. After ten to twenty minutes, begin breathing slowly again, letting go of your prayer word. Close your time with a personal prayer, the Lord's Prayer, a scripture, or inspirational poem. In these moments of centering, we discover that we are always at home with God and that peace is just a moment away.

FIVE

GOSPEL HEALING

*John said to Jesus, "Teacher,
we saw someone casting out demons in your name,
and we tried to stop him,
because he was not following us."
But Jesus said, "Do not stop him;
for no one who does a deed of power in my name
will be able soon afterward to speak evil of me.
Whoever is not against us is for us.
For truly I tell you, whoever gives you a cup of water
to drink because you bear the name of Christ
will by no means lose the reward."*

Mark 9:38–41

*The Tao is like a well:
used but never used up,
It is like the eternal void;
filled with infinite possibilities.*

Tao Te Ching, Chapter Four,
translated by Stephen Mitchell

The Energy of Love is, like the Tao, filled with infinite possibilities. It does not coerce or dominate but opens us to healing energies in every life situation, even when we are facing what can't be cured but must be endured.

Virtually everyone is concerned with healing and wholeness. Physicians like Dr. Oz and Deepak Chopra became international celebrities, whose words are taken as gospel truth by millions. Every afternoon, millions of people receive practical medical advice from four energetic and attractive physicians on *The Doctors*. Scientists are now studying sacred practices and the lifestyles of active churchgoers; they have discovered that "prayer is good medicine" and "religion is good for your health."[14] We are discovering the power of prayer to transform cells as well as souls; spirituality is an essential element of wellness and self-care.

Because healing and wholeness are necessary to everyone's life, we will reflect on spiritual practices for personal healing in the next three chapters: Jesus as a spiritual healer and model for our healing practices; the interplay of faith and medicine; and healing through Reiki touch and community worship.

Jesus is at the heart of my reflections on global healing not only because of my commitment to following the way of Jesus but also because among religious leaders, Jesus stands out in his integration of body, mind, spirit, and relationships. Jesus was truly a prophetic healer, presenting people and communities with alternative visions and inviting them to embody these visions in the creation of healing communities.

The Gospels describe Jesus's many personal and community vocations: he was a storyteller and speaker of parables, a wise teacher, a hospitable friend, and a religious critic. He was also a healer of the whole person, body, mind, spirit, and relationships. In fact, healing was at the heart of his ministry. More than half of the first ten chapters of Mark's Gospel involve healing stories. Explicit narratives of whole-person healing play a major role in the other three Gospels, Matthew, Luke, and John. Jesus saw his vocation as liberating captives, giving sight to the blind, and mediating new energy to persons with handicaps of body, mind, or spirit.

Jesus's healing of the whole person was central to his mission of proclaiming and promoting God's abundant life (John 10:10). While Jesus never taught a methodology of healing, he employed a variety of techniques that still have power today: healing touch, energy work, healing words, prayer, hospitality, acceptance, spittle, and placebo effect. Jesus healed by direct contact, but he also cured from a distance. Jesus's multifactored approach invites us to use the healing techniques that reflect our personality, life experience, setting, and vocation: Eastern energy medicine and Western technology, touch and words, and prayer and pharmaceuticals. Wherever healing is present, God is its source, regardless of the methodology. Jesus's healing gospel embraces the whole Earth, transcending and embracing our particular religious traditions.

Two healing stories serve as a lens through which to experience Jesus's healing ministry and our own calling to be healing companions to one another. Take a moment to read these stories twice in the spirit of lectio divina, or holy reading, listening for God's unique word to you within the words of scripture. If you have the leisure to do so, take a fifteen-minute meditative walk and then journal your inspirations.

When Jesus had crossed again in the boat to the other side, a great crowd gathered around him; and he was by the sea. Then one of the leaders of the synagogue named Jairus came and, when he saw him, fell at his feet and begged him repeatedly, "My little daughter is at the point of death. Come and lay your hands on her, so that she may be made well, and live." So he went with him. And a large crowd followed him and pressed in on him.

Now there was a woman who had been suffering from hemorrhages for twelve years. She had endured much under many physicians, and had spent all that she had; and she was no better, but rather grew worse. She had heard about Jesus, and came up behind him in the crowd and touched his cloak, for she said, "If I but touch his clothes, I will be made well." Immediately her hemorrhage stopped; and she felt in her body that she was healed of her disease. Immediately aware that power had gone forth from him, Jesus turned about in the crowd and said, "Who touched my clothes?" And his disciples said to him, "You see the crowd pressing in on you; how can you say, 'Who touched me?'" He looked all around to see who had done it.

But the woman, knowing what had happened to her, came in fear and trembling, fell down before him, and told him the whole truth. He said to her, "Daughter, your faith has made you well; go in peace, and be healed of your disease." (Mark 5:21–34)

What insights did you receive as you read this story? Where does the story touch and transform your life? How do these two healing stories lure you to experience your own need for healing and wholeness? What steps do you need to experience creative transformation of mind, body, spirit, and relationships?

THE ENERGIES OF LOVE

Sickness and health are physical, spiritual, social, and relational in nature. The woman with the flow of blood was considered spiritually unclean and viewed as a sinner, deserving of her illness, in light of traditional Jewish identification of immorality with illness. A spiritual outcast, her illness prevented her from going to temple. She contaminated everything she touched. She received no pity since her religious tradition assumed that her behavior had led to her illness. Moreover, because of her uncontrolled and chronic bleeding, she could not, if she were married, have intimate relations with her husband. In light of the religious and social stigma, this woman may even have asked herself, "What did I do wrong to be sick?"

Still, despite the ostracism and judgment she experienced, this woman courageously sought out Jesus. She may have realized that encountering the Healer Jesus was her last chance to receive a cure. I suspect that she repeated the following affirmation, or mantra, over and over as she crept toward the Healer: "If I touch him, I will be well. If I touch him, I will be well. If I touch him, I will be well." No doubt her affirmation strengthened her resolve and buoyed her spirits as she experienced the scorn and fear of the townsfolk she passed. Some may even have jeered at her, challenging her to go home and not contaminate the neighborhood with her presence.

In her boldness—unclean touching clean, sinner touching righteous, woman touching man—she reached out and felt a dynamic charge of dynamic energy, mysterious, yet life-transforming. She was cured of her hemorrhage: she felt the energy of love course through body and spirit, illuminating and enlivening her cells and soul.

Her healing arose from two distinct but interdependent sources: her faith and Jesus's healing energy. The healing was relational and many faceted, not individualistic and unilateral. It involved, as most of the Gospel healings suggest, a partnership between Jesus and the persons seeking healing for themselves or others.

This woman's healing encompassed many contemporary healing practices. If she over and over repeated her spiritual affirmation, "If I only touch him, I will be made well," she was using a mantra-like affirmation to guide her steps and bolster her courage. Affirmations have been shown to have both physiological and spiritual effects. Could her affirmation have opened her energy centers (meridians and chakras) to the energy residing in Jesus and her?

In any case, divine energy was released. In this story, Jesus's energy work appears to be unconscious in nature; it simply flowed from the healer to her without any effort on his part. I believe that Jesus's openness to God's healing energy made him a healing source wherever he was and regardless of his conscious intent. The energy of Jesus, demonstrated in this story, seems to me to be similar in kind to the chi or ki, the energy of the universe flowing through our bodies that can be enhanced by various techniques such as Qigong, Tai Chi, and Reiki. It also resembles universal energy, prana, and enlivening the chakras, which is heightened by the practice of yoga.

This healing story implicitly challenges any form of communal ostracism, whether by attitude or behavior. Jesus never blamed or banned the victim. Instead, he saw illness as many faceted and not entirely the result of the quality of our faith, attitudes, or actions. A holistic vision challenges any one-dimensional spiritual theories regarding the causes of illness, such as, "You create your own reality," "Your state of mind creates health and illness," or, "Your faith insures health and prosperity, while continued illness and failure result from your lack of faith."

Our faith can be an important factor in health and prosperity, but our faith is just one factor among many. Since faith may be the tipping point among a multiplicity of causal factors, cultivating a positive attitude and faithful spirit is important for our overall well-being, regardless of whether our illnesses are curable, chronic, or incurable. As a village pastor, I am regularly called upon to pray, often over the telephone as well as in person, for people who are facing matters of life and death or going through difficult personal or professional times. I believe faith can do amazing things—but we cannot blame people for their illness or poverty, or congratulate ourselves for our health and prosperity.

CREATING HEALING CIRCLES

The healing of Jairus's twelve-year-old daughter involves the interplay of faith and unfaith, hope and despair. When Jesus encounters those who believe she is dead and scoff at his open-source diagnosis that she is sleeping, not dead, he throws them out. He only allows those who believe that she can get well to have access to the little girl. He creates a healing circle that evokes and intensifies God's healing energy.

You can become part of someone's healing circle and you can call upon your own healing circle in times of personal need. It takes a village, as the African proverb asserts, to raise a sick child, restore our spirits, or help us die with grace and dignity. It also takes a village of healing friends for many of us to experience physical healing or maintain recovery from addiction, depression, or illness. In the spirit of God's invitation to create circles of healing, let us take a few moments to make this story come alive in our own experience.

While he was still speaking, some people came from the leader's house to say, "Your daughter is dead. Why trouble the teacher any further?" But overhearing what they said, Jesus said to the leader of the synagogue, "Do not fear, only believe." He allowed no one to follow him except Peter, James, and John, the brother of James. When they came to the house of the leader of the synagogue, he saw a commotion, people weeping and wailing loudly. When he had entered, he said to them, "Why do you make a commotion and weep? The child is not dead but sleeping."

And they laughed at him. Then he put them all outside, and took the child's father and mother and those who were with him, and went in where the child was. He took her by the hand and said to her, "Talitha cum," which means, "Little girl, get up!" And immediately the girl got up and began to walk about (she was twelve years of age). At this they were overcome with amazement.

> *He strictly ordered them that no one should know this, and told them to give her something to eat. (Mark 5:35–43)*

As you live with this scripture, finding points of contact with your own or another's needs for healing and wholeness, consider the following questions: To whom are you called to act as a healing presence? Which persons would you call upon if you found yourself in a personal, spiritual, physical, professional, or relational crisis? Can you visualize the persons you have chosen to be part of your healing circle? Through God's grace, you can be the answer to someone's prayer, and other persons, through that same healing grace, can be media of healing for you.

HEALING AND CELEBRATION

Now, at your leisure, take some to go deeper in the story of the raising of Jairus' daughter.

Begin with a moment of prayer, breathing deeply the presence of divine healing energy. Let your imagination wander without judgment or editing. Allow yourself to become the young girl in the coma. What does it feel like to be in a comatose state? Do you have any experiences while you are comatose? Are you aware of the outside world? Do you have any hopes, dreams, or thoughts? Are you in a peaceful state or panicking?

In the midst of this comatose state, you hear a voice whispering in your ear but resonating in your whole being, saying, "Get up." How do you feel about getting up, responding to the call?

You finally open your eyes: Who do you immediately see? What loving persons are there to greet you? Do you see Jesus? If so, what is his appearance? As you come to consciousness, you hear Jesus say to you, "What would you like to eat? What would you like me to prepare for you?" Take a moment to think of what favorite food you would like the Healer to fix for you. Make your request known to Jesus without embarrassment or fear.

In response to your request, Jesus fixes you a meal. Take time to savor it. How does it taste? In conclusion, take some time to give thanks for God's loving care for you and the joy of a good meal.

Healing leads to celebration and affirmation of this good Earth. This young woman's healing is all about enjoying a good meal, experiencing the love of her family, and moving ahead toward future adventures as a young woman. When I do this exercise with spiritual-growth groups, people often need to be coaxed to share what foods they want Jesus to prepare them. But, once they get going, there's joy and laughter in knowing that God appreciates good food too. Recently when I used this exercise the answers were: homemade macaroni and cheese, lobster, filet mignon, strawberry short cake, freshly baked bread, and chocolate mousse with cappuccino. Taste and see, for God is good!

Spiritual growth involves gratitude for the beauties of life and commitment to creating circles of healing whose aim is to insure that everyone can enjoy the fullness of life in mind, body, spirit, relationships, and social involvement.

HEALING AFFIRMATIONS

Jesus's healing ministry invites us to live by the power of affirmative faith. I believe that holistic theology and spirituality involves certain affirmations that shape the way we look at the world and ourselves, that motivate us to life-transforming actions. These affirmations can change your life. They can awaken you to the powers of healing touch, the comfort of healing circles, and the freedom of untrammeled imagination.

> *God wants all people to have abundant life.*
>
> *God wants me to have abundant life.*
>
> *God is at work in our lives in partnership with our love, prayers, and our use of medical care.*
>
> *God is at work in my life in partnership with my love, prayers, and my use of medical care.*
>
> *God works in a world of many causal factors, seeking the best outcome in every situation.*
>
> *God seeks the best outcome for me in every situation.*
>
> *God is concerned with the whole person, mind, body, and spirit.*
>
> *God is concerned with my wholeness, mind, body, and spirit.*

God seeks the healthy and just societies that promote the well-being of all creation.

I have a role as God's partner in healing other persons and the Earth.

Living with these affirmations will transform your life and help you move from passivity to action in times of crisis. They will empower you to become a member of God's healing circle for your companions and this good Earth.

SPIRITUAL OPENINGS

Spiritual texts are meant to be embodied. Whether we read the Bhagavad Gita, Tao Te Ching, I Ching, Quran, Upanishads, Bible, or texts form North American, Australian, Asian, or African aboriginal peoples, we are invited to become part of the text—to see ourselves as Abraham and Sarah, Jesus's mother Mary, Arjuna from the Bhagavad Gita, an aboriginal singer, or a dancing Sufi. We are challenged to claim the lively and imaginative energy of God, residing in these wisdom traditions, that embraces and inspires all faiths, peoples, and creatures.

As always begin your spiritual practice with a time of centering, breathing in God's energetic presence. As you breathe, visualize a healing light entering your body with every breath. Imagine this light filling your whole being, beginning with your head and descending gradually to your toes. With every successive breath, feel yourself becoming progressively filled with God's spirit of healing, filling every cell, organ, and system of your body and restoring your mind. Let this light surround you, cleansing, enlivening, and eliminating any disease. Let this light inspire you to become an energetic being of light and healing.

Now visualize another person—someone in need of God's healing light. Visualize yourself joined with this individual so that every time you exhale, the healing light flowing in and through you fills and surrounds your companion. See this person growing in wholeness and joy, experiencing the fullness of divine healing energy.

Conclude by giving thanks for God's healing light, illuminating every situation, and bringing healing to you, your companion, and all creation.

SIX

SPIRITUALITY, MEDICINE, AND HEALING

And wherever Jesus went, into villages or cities or farms, they laid the sick in marketplaces and begged him that they might touch even the fringe of his cloak, and all who touched it were healed.

Mark 6:56

*Let us give thanks for the fire.
It gives us warmth for our bodies,
and helps us cook our foods.
It is important for our ceremonies and helps us to heal.*

an indigenous peoples' prayer for the Third Chakra, center of vitality, will, and energy, singer-songwriter-spiritual teacher Dawn Avery[15]

*Here in this body are the sacred rivers;
here are the sun and moon
as well as the pilgrimage places....
I have not encountered another temple
as blissful as my own body.*

Saraha, also known as Rahula, eighth-century Buddhist wisdom teacher

The growing interdependence of life is shaping today's emerging global medicine. We have the blessing of Western and non-Western medicines, analysis and intuition, practicality and spirituality, and both high-tech and high-touch approaches to health care, each with its own gifts and approaches to healing and wholeness. When we are seriously ill, we can receive medication, surgery, chemotherapy, and radiation, but we can also take herbs, go to an acupuncturist, receive a Reiki healing touch treatment, or have someone pray for us, anoint us with oil, and ask for God's blessing. Moreover, we are learning that we can prevent illness and promote recovery through meditation as well as medication. Prayer, silence, congregational commitment, and service can transform our cells as well as spirits. We are also discovering that health and healing are global as well as local and that we cannot separate individual health from planetary well-being. We can never fully determine where our bodies end and the world begins in the intricate synergy of life.

Jesus has been described as one of the twin founders of Western medicine. Hippocrates brought analysis, observation, and diagnosis; Jesus brought hospitality, grace, and compassion. Jesus's healing presence changed peoples' souls as well as cells, and transformed their place in society from outcast to fellow citizen. Jesus used saliva and mud, considered first-century medical treatments, as healing sacraments. Today, in Jesus's spirit, we can take our own medications meditatively and prayerfully.

As we saw in the previous chapter, health and illness can be viewed from a variety of perspectives. Sickness is, after all, never just a physical issue. Sickness raises issues of vulnerability, meaning, vocation, inconvenience, dependence, and theology. We often ask: Why is this happening to me? What did I do to deserve this? Will I ever return to health again? Where is God in my pain and suffering, or the pain and suffering of a loved one? Am I responsible for my illness—or is it the result of forces outside my control and not related in any way to my behavior or personal attitudes?

Jesus recognized our responsibility in health and illness, but he never blamed people for their illnesses nor did he see illness as an instrument of divine punishment or teaching device. Jesus affirmed that God wants us to experience joy, health, and Shalom. Jesus did not blame the sight-impaired person for his illness, nor did Jesus assume good fortune was the result of following religious and moral guidelines (John 9:1–12). He affirmed that the sun shined and the rain fell on the righteous or unrighteous alike (Matthew 5:46). He affirmed that God seeks the well-being of all persons—friend and stranger, outcast and socially prominent, foreigner and fellow citizen.

Still, life can be messy. and the tragedies we experience are as much a matter of happenstance as the result of intentionality. In the interdependent nature of life, we must reject any linear acts–consequences understanding of health and illness that assumes we individually reap what we sow, create our own realities, or cause our illnesses by lack of faith or negative attitudes. We have a role in our health and illness, but our role is limited and contextual rather than all determining.

MEDICINE DISCOVERS SPIRITUALITY

Medicine has discovered spirituality, and science is studying the sacred. In recent years, a number of bestselling books have asserted the positive relationship between spirituality and health: *Ageless Body, Timeless Mind* (Deepak Chopra), *The Faith Factor* (Dale Matthews), *Prayer Is Good Medicine* (Larry Dossey), *The Molecules of Emotion* (Candace Pert), and *Timeless Healing* (Herbert Benson).

Recent medical studies, while still preliminary, indicate the following benefits of spiritual practices in overall health:

> Regular practice of meditation (the relaxation response) lowers blood pressure, enhances immune system functioning, and provides deep rest.
>
> Healing touch reduces pain and stress.
>
> Intercessory prayer may support better recovery from certain illnesses.
>
> Church attendance and commitment promotes longevity, positive aging, and better recovery from illness, along with decreased substance abuse.

In partnership with physicians and holistic healers, theologians, pastors, and spiritual healers have also recognized that prayer, meditation, healing touch, laying on of hands, and anointing with oil complement technological medical care.

OTHER HEALERS

Jesus welcomed other healers as well as the initiatives of his own followers. Listen deeply to these healing words as you consider the many healing pathways available today:

> *John said to Jesus: "Teacher, we saw someone casting out demons in your name, and we tried to stop him, because he was not following us." But Jesus said, "Do not stop him: for no one who does a deed of power in my name will be able soon afterwards to speak evil of me. Whoever is not against us is for us. For truly I tell you, whoever gives you a cup of water to drink because you bear the name of Christ will by no means lose the reward." (Mark 9:38–41)*

Consider for a moment the following questions: Where have you experienced healing? What modalities of health care have been most beneficial to you? Are you open to a variety of approaches to healing and wholeness? I believe that wherever healing is present—in a laboratory, sanctuary, healing-touch center, or an operating room—God is its source.

When Susan was diagnosed with cancer, she received the best medical treatment at a National Cancer Institute hospital. Early on, however, she realized that she needed more than chemotherapy; she needed the healing energy that only God could supply. The diagnosis inspired her to go on a spiritual pilgrimage without leaving her Washington, DC, suburb. Knowing my interest in complementary medicine, she sought out my counsel. I suggested that she learn centering prayer, positive affirmations, and visualizations. I also invited her to receive a series of Reiki treatments and offered to teach her Reiki healing touch for her own self-care so that she could give herself treatments on chemotherapy days. Three years after the initial diagnosis, Susan is cancer free; she says, "Once I committed myself to meditation and Reiki, I knew everything would be all right. The chemo worked wonders in eliminating the cancer, but I needed spiritual healing as well. I also needed a sense of calm and well-being to lessen the negative effects of the chemotherapy. Now that I'm on the way to a cure, Reiki, prayer, and affirmations have become everyday companions. I feel better than I have in years!"

PERSONAL HEALING

Listen to another healing story in the spirit of holy reading, reading with your whole persons, opening to divine inspiration in the words of scripture and the wisdom of your life. What words or insights emerge in living with the story of Jesus's healing of a sight-impaired man?

They came to Jericho. As he and his disciples and a large crowd were leaving Jericho, Bartimaeus son of Timaeus, a blind beggar, was sitting by the roadside. When he heard that it was Jesus of Nazareth, he began to shout out and say, "Jesus, Son of David, have mercy on me!" Many sternly ordered him to be quiet, but he cried out even more loudly, "Son of David, have mercy on me!" Jesus stood still and said, "Call him here." And they called the blind man, saying to him, "Take heart; get up, he is calling you." So throwing off his cloak, he sprang up and came to Jesus. Then Jesus said to him, "What do you want me to do for you?" The blind man said to him, "My teacher, let me see again." Jesus said to him, "Go; your faith has made you well." Immediately he regained his sight and followed him on the way. (Mark 10:46–52)

The man's encounter with Jesus is an opportunity for both physical healing and spiritual transformation. Notice that Jesus responds to the man's plea with a question: "What do you want me to do for you?" Jesus respects Bartimaeus's integrity and freedom. Healing is relational, not coercive and unilateral; it expands our agency and creativity. When we claim what we really need, our prayers are more heartfelt, and resources for healing are activated. New energies burst forth to heal body, mind, and spirit.

Bartimaeus needed to see again. He may also have had other needs that he was unaware of until Jesus questioned him.

Reflect a moment with Bartimaeus. If Jesus were to ask you, "What do you want me to do for you?" how would you answer? Would your answer be obvious or multilayered in nature? Beyond the obvious healing foci—physical illness, relational alienation, grief, economic insecurity, and spiritual confusion—do you have deeper needs for God's healing touch?

Television healers often do a disservice to congregational healing services and persons in need of healing. Their programs suggest that all healing is immediate; everyone they pray for is healed; and every prayer is clearly and successfully answered, especially after a financial contribution to their ministries. No failures happen on the healing stage or in front of the camera. Everyone praises God for palpable healing of body, mind, and spirit. Theatrics like this are deceptive—or they may stretch our credulity. In real life, healing is usually much more complex and not always immediate. Many people go home from healing crusades in a variety of conditions: some are truly cured of their ailments, but the majority may temporarily feel better without experiencing a definitive cure; they may find better coping strategies; or they may feel peace with what cannot be changed in a chronic or incurable condition. Sadly, some feel depressed that they were left out of God's healing purposes. If health and illness are the result of many factors, then the television healers' words and theatrics are not omnipotent, but part of a matrix of causes that determine our health and well-being. Whether in a quiet healing service or elaborate televised healing crusade, our prayers and support can often be the catalyst, but not the only factor, that triggers illness and health, panic and peace.

GRADUAL HEALING

In the following healing story, Jesus's approach is a far cry from televangelists' bombastic style. In fact, his healing power is limited for reasons that are left unanswered in the narrative. What do you think the initial response might have been if the following occurred at a highly orchestrated faith healing crusade?

> *They came to Bethsaida. Some people brought a blind man to him and begged him to touch him. He took the blind man by the hand and led him out of the village; and when he had put saliva on his eyes and laid his hands on him, he asked him, "Can you see anything?" And the man looked up and said, "I can see people, but they look like trees, walking." Then Jesus laid his hands on his eyes again; and he looked intently and his sight was restored, and he saw everything clearly. Then he sent him away to his home, saying, "Do not even go into the village." (Mark 8:22–25)*

This story contains a number of insights that help us frame a realistic vision of healing and wholeness.

The healing is gradual not immediate.

Jesus does not blame the man for lack of faith when a cure does not immediately occur.

Jesus uses spittle, an ordinary folk remedy—though also standard first-century medical practice—as a medium of healing.

Jesus persists in prayer, despite mixed results at first.

Jesus's continuous prayer enables the man to see again.

I believe that the Gospel writer included this passage as an image of hope for persons dealing with chronic and incurable ailments, whose prayers often appear to be deferred or unanswered. The story reminds us that diseases that took years to develop may take time for recovery. The story also reveals the importance of persistence as a factor in healing and wholeness: cures do not usually happen immediately and although our faith and health practices, like the use of antibiotics and surgery, can hasten a cure, we often need time to recover and claim a healthier self. Finally, the Gospel tells us that God doesn't give up on our personal and relational healing, and neither should we. God will adjust to apparent "failures" by injecting new energies and possibilities into our lives, congruent with our current physical, emotional, and spiritual condition.

We need to recognize that factors beyond our control always shape the healing process. Our attitudes and the prayers of a healing community make a difference, but they are integrated with other environmental, spiritual, and physiological factors. The following rather curious story from Mark's Gospel notes that even Jesus's healing power was limited by the attitudes of his kinfolk. Still, despite their unbelief, God's providential aim at healing could not be entirely thwarted. Even when we turn away from God's healing vision, God's quest for abundant life is still moving, albeit unconsciously, in our cells and spirits.

He left that place and came to his hometown, and his disciples followed him. On the Sabbath he began to teach in the synagogue, and many who heard him were astounded. They said, "Where did this man get all this? What is this wisdom that has been given to him? What deeds of power are being done by his hands! Is not this the carpenter, the son of Mary and brother of James and Joses and Judas and Simon, and are not his sisters here with us?" And they took offence at him. Then Jesus said to them, "Prophets are not without honor, except in their hometown, and among their own kin, and in their own house." And he could do no deed of power there, except that he laid his hands on a few sick people and cured them. And he was amazed at their unbelief. (Mark 6:1–6)

This story poses the following question: If unbelief can minimize the impact of God's healing energy in our lives and communities, what positive energies might be released if we fully opened to God's healing touch? When I used this passage in a healing seminar, someone noted that this passage, like so many others, "could be used to hurt as well as heal." She went on to say, "When I had serious depression, I was told that if I only trusted God, I would get well. Although I struggled with whether or not to use medication and not just faith and willpower, I came to realize that in saying 'yes' to medication, I was also saying yes to God. I also realized that if I said 'no' to the medications available, I might be standing in the way of God's healing power. I needed prayer and faith, but I also needed medication to be faithful to God's healing promises."

HEALING AND CURING

While there can't always be a cure, there can always be a healing. In today's medical world, the word "cure" involves the cessation of symptoms as well successful treatment of the organic cause of an illness. For example, recently, after using antibiotics, my sinus infection could be described as cured when I had no more symptoms. I can be described as cured from a specific heart ailment after successful bypass surgery or a stent. My son is now considered cured of cancer, since he has had no recurrence in seven years following the conclusion of his chemotherapy treatments.

Healing is a different matter. We can be cured without being healed; we can receive a heart bypass, for example, and continue to practice unhealthy behaviors and eating habits that will contribute to future heart disease. A broken bone can heal, but we can still be frightened of falling and choose not to return to appropriate normal activities. We can also be healed without being cured: we can live in peace with chronic illness or face death trusting that nothing can separate us from the love of God.

As mortals, the ultimate goal in healing is grounded in our relationship with God, the source of all of life's blessings. We can experience the fullness of well-being regardless of our health condition when we trust the promises of another fellow sufferer, the author of Psalm 139:

Where can I go from your spirit?
Or where can I flee from your presence?
If I ascend to heaven, you are there;
if I make my bed in Sheol, you are there.
If I take the wings of the morning
and settle at the farthest limits of the sea,
even there your hand shall lead me,
and your right hand shall hold me fast.
If I say, "Surely the darkness shall cover me,
and the light around me become night,"
even the darkness is not dark to you;
the night is as bright as the day,
for darkness is as light to you.

In living and dying, God is with us, promising that nothing can separate us from his healing love.

SPIRITUAL OPENINGS

The Apostle Paul affirms that our bodies are the temples of God. He counsels us to glorify God with our bodies. Yet, many of us see our bodies mechanistically or as hindrances to our happiness. We have internalized social stereotypes of beauty, which often leave us feeling inferior, embarrassed, or shamed. In this spiritual practice, I invite you to experience the wonder and beauty of mind, body, and spirit, and experience your uniqueness as God's beloved child.

Begin by breathing deeply, awakening to God's loving energy filling you with every breath. Experience this energy within you from head to toe. Filled with God's energy of love, give thanks for your uniqueness as a person. You might make the following prayer: "I thank you God for the wonder of my being," or "I am grateful for who I am." In the stillness of prayer, consider your own unique beauty of mind, body, and spirit. What is holy and beautiful about your embodiment? What is holy about your personality and unique giftedness?

Filled with gratitude for your own unique beauty, make a commitment to care for yourself—body, mind, and spirit—and support the whole-person well-being of others, honoring and bringing forth their beauty, personally, socially, and politically.

Wholeness is relational as well as individual. We cannot separate our own health from the health of those around us. Accordingly, when we appropriately love other peoples' bodies by insuring that they have adequate food, shelter, health care, communal support, and political access, we contribute to our own well-being.

SEVEN

THE ENERGY OF LOVE

*Now there was a woman
who had been suffering from hemorrhages for twelve years.
She had endured much under many physicians,
and had spent all that she had;
and she was no better, but rather grew worse.
She had heard about Jesus,
and came up behind him in the crowd
and touched his cloak, for she said,
"If I but touch his clothes, I will be made well."
Immediately her hemorrhage stopped;
and she felt in her body that she was healed of her disease.
Immediately aware that power had gone forth from him,
Jesus turned about in the crowd and said,
"Who touched my clothes?"
And his disciples said to him,
"You see the crowd pressing in on you;
how can you say, 'Who touched me?'"
He looked all round to see who had done it.
But the woman, knowing what had happened to her,
came in fear and trembling, fell down before him,
and told him the whole truth. He said to her,*

> *"Daughter, your faith has made you well;*
> *go in peace, and be healed of your disease."*
>
> Mark 5:25–34
>
> *You are the light of the world....*
> *Let your light shine.*
>
> Matthew 5:14, 16
>
> *The light which shines in the eye*
> *is really the light of the heart.*
> *The light which fills the heart*
> *is the light of God.*
>
> Rumi, Mathnawi 1126–1127

LIGHTING UP

You are the light of the world—and with illumination comes fire! Deep down each one of us embodies the energy that emerged with the birth of the universe. We are star stuff, giving and receiving the lively energy of divine creative wisdom and healing.

Today, many people are exploring the energy of the universe as it manifests itself in our hands and hearts through complementary healing practices such as acupuncture, massage, Shiatsu, Qigong, Tai Chi, therapeutic touch, and Reiki healing touch. I became a Reiki practitioner in the mid 1980s and have been a Reiki master-teacher since 1990. Reiki healing touch is central to my life as a Christian and as a partner with God in healing the world. God's light shines in and through everyone, and Reiki healing touch, along with many other forms of energy healing and medicine, enables us to let our light shine brightly, bringing healing and wholeness to ourselves and the world around us.

Medical research has found that the many varieties of healing touch are associated with feelings of calm, decreases in blood pressure, pain relief, and stress reduction. Anecdotal evidence associates healing touch with accelerated healing of wounds, enhanced immune functioning, and faster recovery from illness. When we touch another person in love, whether it is caressing an infant, cradling an elder, or embracing our beloved, we are sharing in the omnipresent energy of love from which galaxies, planets, and species burst forth.

Mark's Gospel speaks of a power flowing from Jesus to a woman suffering from a gynecological ailment. Could this power have been the manifestation of the first moment of creation and God's ongoing creativity in the universe? Can we, as Jesus promised his followers, do "greater things" when we align ourselves with the holy energy that inspired his own healing ministry? Can we become, as Martin Luther promised, "little Christs," who mediate divine healing to persons and the planet?

A RENDEZVOUS WITH REIKI

One of my favorite detective programs is *Dragnet*. The iconic Joe Friday often halts what he perceives to be emotionally laden and subjective conversations with the statement, "Just the facts, ma'am." The diligent detective focuses on what he perceives to be purely objective data, unencumbered by personality, meaning, or intentionality. As important as the quest for objectivity may be, however, this is just the beginning and not the end of our quest for spiritual transformation. Philosopher Alfred North Whitehead once asserted that "it is more important that a proposition be interesting than it be true.... For the energy of operation of an occasion of experiences is its interest and is its importance. But of course a true proposition is more apt to be interesting than a false one." In describing the creation of the universe, aboriginal storytellers of all continents often remark, "This may not have happened but this is true." The stories of Adam and Eve, Abraham and Sarah, Jacob and the ladder of angels, and Queen Esther, are life-transforming even if they never occurred as narrated. The same applies to Jesus's parables and the great works of literature. There is a deeper truth, the truth of myth, poetry, symbolism, archetype, and imagination, that surrounds and gives meaning to everyday facts.

Provocative propositions introduce new possibilities and invite us to embark on adventures to new and uncharted frontiers. This is certainly the case with the story of Mikao Usui and the modern origins of Reiki healing touch. There is much controversy about whether Usui was a Christian and practitioner of multiple spiritual paths or a Buddhist whose quest for healing practices within his own spiritual tradition led him to an unexpected mystical experience. In any case, the Reiki story invites us to go beyond facts to discover the energy of love that embraces every wisdom quest.

When I first learned Reiki healing touch in the mid 1980s, I heard the following account of its origins. Mikao Usui (1865–1926) was the prefect, or dean, of a Japanese Christian college and Christian minister. Following a sermon he preached on a healing story from scripture, his students asked him, "Do you believe that Jesus healed people?" When he responded affirmatively, they challenged him to perform a healing. Embarrassed by the distance between his experience and the fiery hands-on faith of Jesus's first followers, Usui embarked on a spiritual pilgrimage that took him to the United States and the University of Chicago Divinity School, where he sought to learn how to become God's healing partner. Disappointed by the lack of interest in healing among his professors and fellow students in America, he returned to Japan and sought out Buddhist healing wisdom. Here, too, he was disappointed. Although healing powers had been attributed to Buddha, none of the Buddhist teachers he encountered saw physical healing as essential to Buddhist practice. In the course of his quest, he discovered a number of Tibetan Buddhist healing texts but no technique for experiencing the healing energy they described. Undeterred in his quest for a pathway to healing, Usui retreated to a mountaintop where he fasted and prayed for twenty-one days. On the twenty-first day, Usui had a mystical experience that transformed his heart, head, and hands forever: a beam of light from the heavens struck him on the forehead, causing him to lose consciousness. Out of this mystical experience, Usui discovered a group of primordial healing symbols and a way to activate their healing powers.

In recent years, this story has been challenged by critics who assert that the first North American Reiki teachers emphasized Usui's Christianity to make it more palatable in the aftermath of Pearl Harbor and World War II. Although there is virtually no documentary evidence to support the story I learned as a Reiki level-one student in the 1980s, I believe that this story is still "true" even if it isn't factual. I believe that the story of Usui's discovery of Reiki healing touch represents the union of East and West, intellect and intuition, mysticism and action, Buddhist insight and Christian compassion, and mind and body. It points to a universal divine energy, flowing through all things, manifested in many ways, and always aiming at wholeness. It is the energy of Jesus's healing touch, a parent caressing a newborn, and an adult child holding a dying parent. It is the energy that comforts a crying child and embraces a beloved elder. It is the energy that heals cells and souls alike, whether it comes through Christian laying on of hands, a Native North American blessing, an African Yoruba prayer, a Shamanic incantation, or a Hindu mantra. Healing takes many forms, and global wisdom looks for enlightening energy wherever it may be found.

TRANSFORMING TOUCH

Touch can transform our bodies, minds, and spirits. Through the practice of Reiki and Christian laying on of hands, I have learned that everyone, regardless of health, age, or religious tradition, can share in God's healing light. Others have found this same healing touch in medical qigong, therapeutic touch, Pentecostal prayer, massage, chiropractic, acupuncture, and acupressure. We are created for healing touch. "It is not good for a person to be alone," the Hebrew scriptures proclaim. We are made for sensuality and sexuality, and for relationships that involve body as well as spirit. The Christian vision of incarnation is an invitation to imagine a "God with skin." The Psalms invite us to "taste and see" the goodness of God in the world of embodiment, in our wonderfully made bodies and the orderly movements of the heavens.

The spirit is embodied and the body is inspired. Physicists and ancient teachers alike affirm that embodiment is energetic and spirit-filled. The days of Descartes's mind-body dualism, conveniently but disastrously separating spirit and flesh, while giving custody of the spirit to faith and the body to science, have given way to a re-enchanted universe of lively energy events and interdependent systems, all reflecting the deep-down and subtle movements of Spirit.

Whether we invoke the language of quantum physics or images of chi, prana, meridians, and chakras, we live, move, and have our being in an energetic universe.

Agnes Sanford, whose healing ministry revived interest in healing among mainstream Christians, asserted that the universe is filled with the energy of God but the "infinite [and energetic] God cannot help us unless we are prepared to receive it into ourselves."[16] Sanford believed that "opening to God's energy is as simple as breathing."[17] Today, scientists such as Candace Pert affirm the same dynamic interdependence of mind, body, and spirit that can promote healing and wholeness. The "molecules of emotion," discovered by Pert, reflect an ever-present biochemical link between mind and body. Mind and body cannot be conveniently separated by a philosopher's ruminations. Intelligence is found in the brain and also in our digestive, immune, and nervous systems. As Candace Pert asserts, the mind is present everywhere in the body.

Christian healers proclaim that the dynamic call-and-response between God and humankind is found in our cells as well as our souls, and that opening to the divine energy within and around us can transfigure our physical lives and transform our minds. In fact, in a universe reflecting divine energy and wisdom in every molecule—this is what it means for God to be omnipresent—we cannot separate mind, body, and spirit; science and spirituality; or facts from subjectivity.

The integration of prayer, meditation, and Reiki healing touch is central to my personal and relational life. Every morning as I walk on the Craigville Beach on Cape Cod, I combine opening to the beauties of the environment with intercessory prayers, affirmations, and distant Reiki. I typically "send" Reiki energy to my family and church congregation, whose steeple I first glimpse as I turn around to return to my car, and to a number of friends who are dealing with crises of mind, body, or spirit. In reality, I am not "sending" the energy from one place to another. In a world of nonlocal relationships, I am simply opening the door for expressions of greater divine healing energy in their lives.

Just a few minutes ago, I received a phone call from a former colleague who is in the middle of chemotherapy treatments for ovarian cancer. After I prayed with her in Jesus's name, asking for healing and peace, I asked her to rest a few minutes while I hung up the phone and returned to my study to give her a distant Reiki treatment. Despite the debilitation she felt after her first cycle of chemotherapy, she was immediately able to get up, shower, dress, and begin to do a little work around the house. I cannot fully attribute this to prayer and Reiki, but I believe that the synergy of prayerful energy and her sense that someone was praying energetically for her enlivened her whole being and activated what scientists call the placebo effect—the impact of our beliefs—to promote healing and wholeness. I also believe that the Reiki healing energy from my distant treatment awakened and enhanced the healing presence of God at the cellular and spiritual levels of her experience.

Reiki healing touch reminds us that we can always do something to support the well-being of others. This morning on my daily walk, I spiritually connected with a good friend who is being treated for an incurable cancer. I placed him in the center of God's love by sending Reiki and healing prayers on his behalf. I have given my friend, along with several others, a gentle distant Reiki treatment every morning since. Could Reiki and prayer have enhanced his overall well-being and extended his lifespan years beyond his original prognosis? I believe so. I believe that along with other health and environmental factors, Reiki healing touch and prayer, and his awareness of being the subject of my prayers, created a sense of loving connection that enhanced his physical and spiritual well-being. It may even have been a watershed moment in his quest for wholeness of body, mind, and spirit. At the very least, my daily practices remind him and others for whom I "intercede" that they are never alone but always surrounded by a circle of healing.

At this point, I must restate my belief that health and illness are the result of many factors, including our overall health condition and our prayers, energy work, and affirmative faith. I believe that our energies, manifested in prayer and Reiki, mingle with God's healing energy to awaken a greater sense of calm and comfort. Even if the practices of prayer and energy work were found to have only minimal value, I would continue these practices to promote greater connection with those for whom I pray and as a reflection of my belief that in the spirit of the butterfly effect, small changes may lead to great results.

Reiki is prayer with our hands. I give daily hands-on Reiki treatments, usually "spot" treatments, to my wife as we watch television, read beside each other, or lie in bed. I give Reiki treatments to my grandchildren as they sleep or sit on my lap. I want to repeat: Reiki is prayer with our hands and reflects my vision of a God with skin, connecting us with each other as members of God's healing circle.

In a typical hands-on Reiki treatment, I lightly touch another person and effortlessly join that individual with the divine source of healing and wholeness. There is no single typical Reiki experience: sometimes my hands feel hot, other times normal. Sometimes the person receiving the Reiki treatment experiences a keen and lively energy flow; other times the experience brings a greater sense of peace but no palpable feelings of warmth. Reiki and other forms of laying on of hands address our needs in affirmative ways, calming our spirits and often awakening healing within our bodies.

Reiki and other forms of healing touch are acts of service, practiced solely for the benefit of those with whom we share God's energy of love. This demands the highest ethical standards, personal integrity, and self-care. We are here solely to be healing partners, sharing God's loving energy to heal persons and the planet. In my case, I have made a commitment to use my hands only to bring beauty, love, and healing to the world. Although I am not an absolute pacifist, my practice of Reiki as a follower of Jesus challenges me to seek peace and reconciliation interpersonally and globally. When we practice Reiki, we can always do something to change our immediate life circumstances and the circumstances of others, and this gives us hope in challenging times: when a cure is not possible, there can always be a healing, grounded in our experiences of connection with God and one another.

SPIRITUAL OPENINGS

My daily spiritual practices include meditation, intercession, the use of affirmations, and walking prayer. I also give myself a daily Reiki treatment, lasting about ten minutes. I believe that self-care includes loving yourself along with your neighbor. As we love ourselves in our wholeness, we can love others more authentically, persistently, and creatively. Filled with God's healing energy, we have the resources to share that energy over the long haul, whether through healing touch and prayer, social action, companionship in crisis and chronic illness, or care for family members.

Even if you do not know a particular practice of energy work, you can still love yourself and your body and draw upon God's ever-flowing stream of healing energy. In this exercise, you can nurture your own well-being by healing touch.

Set aside ten minutes or so for this healing touch treatment. Begin by lying down on a sofa, bed, or floor, breathing deeply and opening to God's energy of love. Place your hands on your body in the following places, corresponding to energy centers identified by the world's religious traditions. While doing so, you may choose to breathe slowly and gently, opening yourself to God's unconditional and transformative love.

1. *top of your head*
2. *forehead*
3. *eyes and sinuses*
4. *throat*
5. *heart*
6. *abdomen/stomach*
7. *genital area*

Experience the peace and energy that comes from being connected to the infinite energy of the universe. God who is fully present throughout the universe is also fully present in your body, mind, and spirit. You are the light of the world: God's creative and healing light flows in and through you.

EIGHT

THE POWER OF AFFIRMATIVE SPIRITUALITY

*Finally beloved, whatever is true,
whatever is honorable, whatever is just,
whatever is pure, whatever is pleasing,
whatever is commendable, if there is any excellence
and anything worthy of praise,
think about these things.*

Philippians 4:8

Right mindfulness or right thinking.

The Seventh Step on Gautama Buddha's
Eightfold Path

A HOLISTIC BIBLE

It often comes as a surprise to people that I am a progressive, global Christian, committed to creative interspirituality, who also finds inspiration, solace, and transformation in the Hebrew and Christian scriptures. Many people see progressive and global Christianity as having gone beyond the words of scripture in search of deeper, more universal truths. In contrast, I believe that the local can also be global, and that the poetry and stories of scripture reflect the ongoing dialogue between God and humankind, always historical and contextual, yet always pointing us to places where we may discover the deepest truths of ourselves and God's world. I see the Hebrew-Christian scriptures as inclusive and evolutionary in nature, the beginning of our spiritual journeys, and not the final resting place and arbiter of truth and falsehood.

Scripture is a living document that invites us to come alive spiritually. A library of contrasting yet interdependent and perspectival revelations, scripture is an adventure book inviting us to explore God's call to our own adventure in our lives. The Bible is a book of affirmations, not unbending rules and doctrines, whose purpose is to help us see the world in terms of abundance, grace, and healing. Though the written canon—the approved texts of scripture—was closed early in the Christian journey, God is still speaking, and there is always more illumination to burst forth on the human adventure. I assume that this is the case for all the world's scriptures: finite and human, they nevertheless reflect God's presence and wisdom, constantly emerging in the lives of persons and institutions.

In this chapter, we will continue our reflections on spiritual practices—in this case affirmative statements—that can transform mind, body, and spirit by meditating on Philippians 4:4–9 as a model for institutional and individual spiritual transformation. The Philippian story begins with a mystical experience. Paul has a vision of a man calling to him to go to Asia Minor. The early Christian movement treasured visions, so Paul's cohorts pay attention to the wisdom Paul receives and after a time of prayerful reflection, they go forth on an adventure to Neapolis and then to Philippi, a city named after Philip of Macedon, father of Alexander the Great. As usual, Paul gets into trouble, starts a community, goes forth on further adventures of good news sharing, and cares for this beloved community from a distance, sharing wise counsel through epistles delivered by his companions in faith.

LIVED SPIRITUALITY

The Philippian journey begins with words of gratitude and hope. There is a gentle providence at work in the life of the community, and this providence will not be deterred by persecution and challenge.

> *I thank my God every time I remember you, constantly praying with joy in every one of my prayers*

for you, because of your sharing of the gospel from the first day until now. I am confident of this, that the one who began a good work among you will bring it to completion by the day of Jesus Christ.... And this is my prayer, that your love may overflow more and more with knowledge and full insight to help you determine what is best, so that on the day of Christ you may be pure and blameless, having produced the harvest of righteousness that comes through Jesus Christ for the glory and praise of God. (Philippians 1:3–6, 9–11)

This passage is chock-full of theological affirmations—short statements that shape our vision of ourselves and the world—that can transform your life and the life of your community.

Take a moment to meditate on these affirmations or repeat them out loud or in a group:

God is doing a good work in my life.

God is doing a good work in our community and congregation.

God's vision of my life will be fulfilled.

God's vision for our community will be fulfilled.

My love is overflowing with knowledge and insight.

Our community's love is overflowing with knowledge and insight.

I am [we are] producing a harvest of righteousness and beauty.

Paul had a strong sense of divine providence. He believed God was working in all things and seeking our well-being throughout the course of our lifetimes. Even in prison, where Paul dictated this letter, he still believed God was directing his path and furthering the spread of the gospel. How could Paul keep from singing when he knew that God was near, his life was in God's hands, God was inspiring his work as an apostle, and nothing could separate him from God's love?

Philippians 2:5–11 continues this vision of God's providential movements in Paul's life and in the world. His writing exhibits what Gautama Buddha described as "right mindfulness."

Let the same mind be in you that was in Christ Jesus, who, though he was in the form of God, did not regard equality with God as something to be exploited, but emptied himself, taking the form of a slave, being born in human likeness. And being found in human form, he humbled himself and became obedient to the point of death—even death on a cross. Therefore God also highly exalted him and gave him the name that is above every name, so that at the name of Jesus every knee should bend, in heaven and on earth and under the earth, and every tongue should confess that Jesus Christ is Lord, to the glory of God the Father.

Our good work is grounded in God's good work in Christ, whose life reflects the adventures of an all-embracing, noncompetitive God. God "rules"—as does Christ—not by coercion or unilateral power but through relationship and love, and by becoming our companion in joy and suffering. When Paul's listeners heard this passage, they had an obvious alternative image in mind and that was Caesar, who ruled with an iron hand, rewarding obedience but punishing anyone who questioned his authority or whose creativity brought new and different ideas into the world. In contrast to the fearful bowing Caesar demanded, Christ rules by love: every knee bends out of thanksgiving and wonder at God's amazing love for creation.

PARTNERSHIP IN SPIRITUAL TRANSFORMATION

The Philippian journey calls us to partnership, not passivity: we are to work out our salvation, our healing process, with fear and trembling—awe and energy—because God's grace inspires and supports us. We are called to be creative partners with God, living in a dynamic conversation in which God wants us to claim our creativity and freedom to embody God's vision of Shalom in our own unique way. God wants us to shine like stars in the heavens, giving light and love to all around us.

The Letter to the Philippians provides a vision of hope for us and our communities. Regardless of our past, we can look forward to a glorious future, pressing ahead toward God's vision for us and the world. The past is not a limitation, nor are we bound by yesterday's faith. The past serves as a springboard for new forms of faithfulness to God and the world. God lures us beyond past achievements to new possibilities of personal and community transformation. The spiritual heart of Philippians is found in these words:

> *Rejoice in the Lord always; again I will say, Rejoice. Let your gentleness be known to everyone. The Lord is near. Do not worry about anything, but in everything by prayer and supplication with thanksgiving let your requests be made known to God. And the peace of God, which surpasses all understanding, will guard your hearts and your minds in Christ Jesus.*
>
> *Finally, beloved, whatever is true, whatever is honorable, whatever is just, whatever is pure, whatever is pleasing, whatever is commendable, if there is any excellence and if there is anything worthy of praise, think about these things. Keep on doing the things that you have learned and received and heard and seen in me, and the God of peace will be with you. (4:4–9)*

Joy is neither an accident nor the result of good fortune or temporary success, but a sustained experience of God's presence in our lives. Because God is near, we can sing hymns of faith in every circumstance of life. Philippians gives us life-changing personal and congregational practices:

>gentleness
>
>prayer for our needs
>
>prayers for others' well-being
>
>gratitude
>
>cultivating an attitude of joy in all circumstances
>
>living affirmatively

Gautama Buddha's vision of right thought and right mindfulness is surely embodied in the word, penned by the Apostle Paul five centuries after Buddha taught the Eightfold Path to freedom to his followers. Spiritual transformation involves an affirmative spirituality, using positive statements repeatedly that can change your life, moving persons and institutions from hopelessness to hope, scarcity to abundance, and alienation to reconciliation. Paul tells his readers, then and now, to live affirmatively—in other words, to practice right mindfulness—by thinking "about these things," nourishing your spirit with healthy soul food rather than superficial or hazardous fast food.

Paul tells us that what we focus on shapes our perception of the events of our lives and our own sense of self-worth. We must confess that many of us have negative scripts we use on a regular basis to describe ourselves such as: "I'm too old," "I can't do that," "I'm not smart,"

"I'm not interesting," "No one will ever love me," "I don't have enough time or money to achieve my goals." Paul grounds his affirmations in the belief that because God's abundant life is flowing through us, we can respond to life's challenges and do great things. Our minds can be transformed and we can become new creations, enlivened by the resurrected Christ.

SPIRITUAL OPENINGS

Listen to these Philippian affirmations. More than that, repeat them over and over until they take root in your life. Let them be the lens through which you interpret the events of your life.

> *The good work God has begun in my life God will bring to fullness and it will be a harvest of righteousness.*
>
> *I have the mind of Christ.*
>
> *I am working out my salvation in partnership with God.*
>
> *I shine like a star in the heavens.*
>
> *I am running the race, looking toward God's vision for my life.*
>
> *I can do all things through Christ who strengthens me.*
>
> *My God will supply all my needs.*

Each of the world's great religious tradition invites its followers to follow affirmative spirituality. Hindus greet one another with the words "Namaste." As I bow to others, I honor and great the divine spark in them. My divine spark greets their divine spark. From this affirmative greeting, we can formulate the following life-transforming affirmations:

I am joined with the divinity in everyone

My divine spark shines and gives light to everyone I meet.

The Hindu holy book the Upanishads proclaims *Tat Tvam Asi*, "Thou art That": divine reality is your deepest nature. In this spirit, you can live by the following affirmations:

I am holy and divine.

God's reality speaks in and through me.

I participate in God's wholeness.

Everyone I meet shares in God's wholeness.

One of my favorite First Nations' sayings is, "With beauty all around me, I walk."

This affirmation can be articulated in many ways, including:

I walk in beauty everywhere.

I see God's beauty in all things.

I bring beauty to every situation.

In the course of the day, take time to repeat one or more of the following spiritual affirmations from the Christian scriptures. You may also choose to repeat one of the previously described affirmations from the Hindu or First Nations' traditions.

> *I am the light of the world.*
>
> *God's light shines in and through me.*
>
> *I am created in God's image.*
>
> *I am God's beloved child.*
>
> *Nothing can separate me from the love of God.*
>
> *God's healing energy flows in and through me.*
>
> *God will supply all my needs.*
>
> *God speaks to me in every encounter.*
>
> *All things are possible when I open to God's vision.*

Repeat these affirmations throughout the day, especially when you are tempted to negative thinking or self-talk.

Affirmations do not deny our limitations or current health or economic condition; they awaken us to a deeper understanding and experience of ourselves and God's presence in our lives. They open us to a deeper realism from which surprising and unexpected healing energies arise.

NINE

CONTEMPLATION AND ACTION

God is our refuge and strength,
a very present help in trouble.
Therefore we will not fear,
though the earth should change,
though the mountains shake in the heart of the sea;
though its waters roar and foam,
though the mountains tremble with its tumult.
There is a river whose streams make glad the city of God,
the holy habitation of the Most High.
God is in the midst of the city; it shall not be moved;
God will help it when the morning dawns....
The LORD of hosts is with us;
the God of Jacob is our refuge....
"Be still, and know that I am God!
I am exalted among the nations,
I am exalted in the earth."
The LORD of hosts is with us;
the God of Jacob is our refuge.

from Psalm 46

> God said, "Go out
> and stand on the mountain before the LORD,
> for the LORD is about to pass by."
> Now there was a great wind,
> so strong that it was splitting mountains
> and breaking rocks in pieces before the LORD,
> but the LORD was not in the wind;
> and after the wind an earthquake,
> but the LORD was not in the earthquake;
> and after the earthquake a fire,
> but the LORD was not in the fire;
> and after the fire a sound of sheer silence.
> When Elijah heard it, he wrapped his face in his mantle
> and went out and stood at the entrance of the cave.
> Then there came a voice to him that said,
> "What are you doing here, Elijah?"
>
> 1 Kings 19:11–13

DYNAMIC SPIRITUALITY

The visionary thinking described in this book is not esoteric or irrelevant, but practical and life-changing when applied to the tasks of everyday living. Our theological visions are meant to be embodied in the complexities of daily life and political decision-making. What we believe should take root and shape our family lives, relationships, occupations, and political involvement.

Healthy, lively theology affirms a vision of reality that celebrates creativity, embodiment, imagination, and adventure. It proclaims a gospel of interdependent creativity in which God is the primary inspiration for the creative process. As the United Church of Christ affirmation proclaims, "God is still speaking!" This wisdom echoes in the voice of the Holy One of Israel, "Behold I do a new thing," and the Reformation affirmation, "The Reformation is constantly reforming." Faithfulness to the Lively One calls us forward, plunging us into the maelstrom of economics, ecology, and politics, as well as the daily tasks of parenting, making a living, job hunting, securing a mortgage, and preparing for retirement.

A holistic vision of reality that shapes our personal and community commitments can be articulated in a handful of life-changing affirmations:

God wants us to do greater things than we can imagine.

Divine possibilities expand as we stretch our wings, imagining new possibilities for ourselves and the world and bringing them to pass in partnership with God.

We are partners with God in healing the world.

Our parenting, politics, and personal priorities matter to God and give texture to God's presence in the world.

God experiences the joy and pain of our lives, especially the lives of vulnerable persons and species, and seeks healing and wholeness in every situation.

In this chapter, we will explore healthy activism, recognizing that both laypersons and spiritual leaders need to receive nurture and guidance for the challenges of their callings. Self-care is not optional for parents or prophets but essential to healthy relational and social involvement over the long haul. Apart from an encounter with the Wellspring of relationships, our personal lives will wither, dry up, and burn out. We will distance ourselves emotionally from our loved ones and the persons for whom we advocate in the political, communal, and interpersonal realms.

Self-care is at the heart of our domestic and political responsibilities, joining the inner and the outer, and the contemplative and active journeys of mission and outreach. Self-care is a form of prayer and mirrors the wisdom of the Jewish teachers and Jesus: "You are to love your neighbor as yourself." As God's beloved children, we love God as we seek wholeness for ourselves and others; we give God a world of beauty, vibrancy, and affirmation. Loving yourself means opening to your own well-being to experience the energy and joy necessary to be open to the well-being of others, whether family members, coworkers, or persons in need.

LIVING IN THE SPIRIT

Let us once again begin with the energetic breath of the Spirit. As John's Gospel proclaims, Jesus breathed on them and said "Receive the Holy Spirit." Today, Jesus still breathes on us, and we can receive God's enlivening, enlightening, and energizing Spirit.

Close your eyes. Take a deep breath, filling yourself with divine energy. Exhale now, letting go of any dis-ease, stress, or burden. Visualize each breath filling you with energy, calm, health, and vision. Experience this holy energy filling you, surrounding you, nurturing you, and protecting you.

In the stillness, remember that God's voice is constantly whispering within us with "sighs too deep for words." Listen in the stillness, asking for a word of wisdom or spiritual guidance for your life today.

Experience God's peace and presence, giving you all the time, energy, and insight you need to serve God, fulfill your dreams, and bring health to your community and the world.

Awaken to the infinite "yes" that gives birth to each moment of life. You are alive, sustained moment by moment by the energy of the universe moving in and through you. Your "yes" to life inspires creativity, courage, and compassion. It opens your senses to divine wonder and to your role in bringing beauty to every life you touch.

THE CHALLENGE OF BEING BUSY

It has been said that busyness is of the devil or, even more drastically, busyness is the devil! We are often busy people, overscheduled, always texting and consulting our iPhones, going from one appointment to the next, and cramming our lives with too many demands and expectations. Even our children are overprogrammed, unable to stand still, entertain themselves, and enjoy the leisure of a summer day with no activities and nowhere to be but right here and right now! With too many demands, we scurry about like the White Rabbit of *Alice's Adventures in Wonderland*, muttering as much to ourselves as anyone else, "I'm late, I'm late, for a very important date."

If someone were to ask us, "What's so important?" we might be at a loss for words. When we are too busy and overbooked, we can lose touch with our spiritual and emotional wellsprings; we can feed others and go through the motions of being good parents, partners, and providers, while suffering from spiritual and emotional malnutrition ourselves. We can do all the right things and say all the right words, but not be present to the sacrament of this unique moment in time. We forget the model of the on-the-go Jesus, who also took time to nurture his spirit and relationships through times of prayer and retreat.

SPIRITUAL OPENINGS

Listen to the following biblical story in the spirit of *lectio divina*, opening yourself to divine insight and inspiration relating to your present life situation. In the narrative, the disciples have recently returned from their first preaching mission without Jesus's supervision; they are elated but fatigued. Their success has created a following and now there are so many demands and so little time to respond to the pain of the world that they are near the breaking point in terms of spiritual, emotional, and physical exhaustion. Burnout is just around the corner. Moreover, in their absence, Jesus's spiritual friend and lifelong companion John the Baptist has been murdered by Herod. No doubt the healer and teacher is grieving and in need of time for his own healing.

> *The apostles gathered around Jesus, and told him all that they had done and taught. He said to them, "Come away to a deserted place all by yourselves and rest a while." For many were coming and going, and they had no leisure even to eat. And they went away in the boat to a deserted place by themselves. Now many saw them going and recognized them, and they hurried there on foot from all the towns and arrived ahead of them. As he went ashore, he saw a great crowd; and he had compassion for them, because they were like sheep without a shepherd; and he began to teach them many things. When it grew late, his disciples came to him and said, "This is a deserted*

place, and the hour is now very late; send them away so that they may go into the surrounding country and villages and buy something for themselves to eat." But he answered them, "You give them something to eat." They said to him, "'Are we to go and buy two hundred denarii worth of bread, and give it to them to eat?" And he said to them, "How many loaves have you? Go and see." When they had found out, they said, "Five, and two fish." Then he ordered them to get all the people to sit down in groups on the green grass. So they sat down in groups of hundreds and of fifties. Taking the five loaves and the two fish, he looked up to heaven, and blessed and broke the loaves, and gave them to his disciples to set before the people; and he divided the two fish among them all. And all ate and were filled; and they took up twelve baskets full of broken pieces and of the fish. Those who had eaten the loaves numbered five thousand men [and no doubt as many women and children as well]. Immediately he made his disciples get into the boat and go on ahead to the other side; to Bethsaida, while he dismissed the crowd. After saying farewell to them, he went up on the mountain to pray. (Mark 6:30–46)

Take a few minutes to respond to the following questions: What wisdom did you receive from this passage? In what ways does it invite you to balance action and contemplation, and rest and activity, as a parent, grandparent, politically active citizen, and friend?

I believe that this passage is a treasure trove of insight for activists of all kinds, domestic and political. The disciples, as a result of their success, are so busy that they have little time for healthy eating habits—they eat on the run, grabbing fast food when they need soul food. They are running on empty, despite their desire to be of service to others. Despite the obvious human needs, Jesus takes the disciples out on a retreat—they go to a deserted place to eat, to play, to pray, and to be rejuvenated. Intense work needs to be balanced by prayer and rest. Human need will never cease, but if we are to be effective over the long haul, we need to care for our spiritual, emotional, physical, relational, and emotional well-being. Refreshed by his retreat, Jesus then has compassion on the needy crowd. Rest, prayer, retreat, meditation, and recognition of our limits are the best antidote for "compassion fatigue," the burnout created by the interplay of idealism, high expectations, long hours, and the emotional wear and tear of working with persons in need. Jesus's retreat also nurtures his imagination: despite their inadequate provisions, he imagines the crowd being fed and then empowers his followers to bring forth a great feast from five loaves and two fish. Finally, Jesus frames a challenging day of teaching, preaching, and pastoral ministry with times of prayer. He begins with retreat, and then, after he dismisses the crowd and his team, he goes to a deserted place to pray.

If you have a few minutes now—or at a later time—bathe your spirit in the following imaginative spiritual practice:

Breathe . . . relax . . . place yourself in the following situation: You have been faithful to God's call, but you are also worn out from the challenges of your work. You have been flourishing in your daily life but despite your successes, each day is draining energetically and emotionally. Noting your fatigue, Jesus invites you on a spiritual retreat on his sailboat.

Take a moment to consider your personal and professional successes and challenges.

As you take this retreat with Jesus, what is your greatest need? Does anyone go with you on the retreat? If so, who are your companions?

Visualize the beauty of the lake and the companionship of your friends. What occurs on your retreat—what wisdom does Jesus share with you? Does Jesus share a spiritual practice to deepen your relationship with God and refresh your spirit?

It is a time for a break in Jesus's seminar, and he is an excellent cook. What does he prepare for you? Visualize yourself and your companions rejoicing in good food and good companionship.

Enjoy your time together, and give thanks for God's refreshing presence in your life. Experience God's bounty sustaining your energetically and spiritually.

You see the shore in the distance, and notice people in great need waiting there. What gift from the retreat do you have to share with them? In what ways are you revived by the retreat experience?

Conclude with a few moments of thanksgiving. Make a commitment to live your retreat experience in the day ahead.

Activity needs to be balanced by contemplation, busyness finds meaning in rest, and words gain gravitas by silence. Whether we live our lives out loud in the public sphere or spend our days caring for children, what we do makes a difference in the world. We cannot underestimate the significance of domestic life—diapers, bedtime stories, homework, and spiritual guidance to our children—to the healing of the planet. Jewish mysticism proclaims that if you save one soul, you save the world. Your well-being and the well-being of the children in your life are essential to saving the Earth. Your advocacy for one child, sold into the sex worker trade, along with thousands of others, to support her or his family, or others robbed of childhoods as a result of working in sweatshops, can transform the world. Loving parents, grandparents, and teachers plant more seeds of global transformation than gridlocked politicians.

All life is political, involving decisions based on our values and priorities, and each action we take influences the larger environment. All vocations, whether public or private, contribute to the health or disease of *society*. Your prayers and spiritual practices, initiated in private, radiate across the planet and plant seeds of healing amid the maelstrom of conflict and polarization.

Franciscan priest and wisdom-giver Richard Rohr poses the following questions for spiritual discernment: "How can I see and use my reflections to expand and not contract? How can I listen for God and learn God's voice, more than God's precise name or plan? How can I keep my mind, heart, and soul open 'in hell'?" To which I would add: How can I remain openhearted, open-minded, and open-spirited in the routine and daily tasks of parenting, professional life, and political involvement? Rohr's response is that an early form of spiritual teaching should involve "not *what* to see nearly as much as *how* to see."[18] In this spirit, spiritual teacher Susan Trout invites us to "see differently," that is, to have a transformed vision of ourselves and the world.[19] Thich Nhat Hanh advises us to breathe deeply, experience calm, and radiate peace. In mindfulness emerging from calm breathing, we discover that "peace is every step."

In this spiritual opening, simply wake up to the wonder of each person you encounter.

In the course of your day, move gently, breathing intentionally between each task. Pause a moment to notice the faces of your spouse or your partner, a child, companion, a fellow traveler on the subway or commuter train, a coworker, or a student. Experience them just for a moment, looking for the holiness within them, the inner light often hidden from our sight and from them as well. Pause to bless each one you encounter.

The time you spend pausing, noticing, and blessing is not "one more thing" to do in the course of the day; instead, it is the way you spend your day and experience the holy otherness of the people you meet. You can also extend this vision to the nonhuman world, bathing yourself in the wonder of all life around you.

TEN

SPIRITUALITY AND SOCIAL JUSTICE

*He has told you, O mortal, what is good;
and what does the LORD require of you
but to do justice, and to love kindness,
and to walk humbly with your God.*

Micah 6:8

*Be just, for justice is closer to God
than consciousness.*

Quran 5:8[20]

EMBODIED SPIRITUALITY

In the previous chapter, we discussed the relationship between action and contemplation and found that domestic life and political involvement gain wisdom, prudence, and persistence when they are spiritually undergirded. While the exact details need to be worked out in our time and place, persons of spirit are challenged to live prophetically. We are called to live according to an alternative social and ethical vision from the norms of our culture. This alternative vision can be related to finances, social involvement, environmental concern, consumption, sacrificial living, and peace-seeking. Planetary survival is under siege and our spirituality must inspire healing actions to insure beauty and well-being for our children's children and the wondrous diversity of flora and fauna.

The Jewish and Christian traditions are inspired by the vision of Shalom, the peaceable realm of God. This vision describes lion and lamb living in harmony, swords beaten into plowshares, joyful households, and laughter being the predominate sound of city life. Buddhism speaks of compassion as the supreme spiritual virtue, lived out in the principles of the Eightfold Path. Hinduism recognizes the divinity of all people as the foundation of ethical behavior. Islam affirms "Dar-as-Salam," or "house of peace," as it highest ideal, and recognizes that the quest for peace and justice should be the goal of persons and communities. We are always, as the Christian scriptures asserts, entertaining angels unaware, and we need to treat all people as if they were Christ in disguise, whether they are standing right in front of us or influenced at a distance by our economic and political decisions. Visions of the peaceable realm are always imaginative in nature and challenge us to affirm the interdependence and unity of all life, despite the apparent differences of gender, sexuality, economics, and nationality.

The alternative (and radical) vision of the prophets and Jesus is that God is concerned with the details of our lives; our treatment of the poor, our business practices, our care for oceans and soils, and our nation's foreign policy all matter to God, because they concern persons and creatures created in God's image and reflecting divine creative wisdom. The prophets believed that we could not truly worship God—indeed, our worship would be hollow—if we turned our backs to the poor. This issue is especially relevant in light of the business practices that led to this century's economic meltdowns, the growing gap between rich and poor, the proliferation of sweatshops and the sex trade, child refugees, and consumption that is oblivious of the future of the planet and the realities of human-created climate change. What we do matters because it brings joy and pain to others, and also joy and pain to God. God is not aloof but feels the anguish of the abused, vulnerable, oppressed, and marginalized. Our Earth care has economic, climate, and political consequences, and it challenges us to honor the planet as our spiritual Mother, indeed, the embodiment of Divine Wisdom, Sophia, described throughout the Bible.

If we turn our backs on the poor and the battered nonhuman world, we will soon no longer be able to experience God, despite our elaborate worship services.

The time is surely coming, says the Lord GOD,
when I will send a famine on the land;
not a famine of bread, or a thirst for water,
but of hearing the words of the LORD.
They shall wander from sea to sea,
and from north to east;
they shall run to and fro, seeking the word of the LORD,
but they shall not find it. (Amos 8:11)

This warning, addressed to Israel's upper-class property owners, was grounded in God's desire for justice and God's anger at injustices committed against the most vulnerable members of society. The prophet is clear that the profit motive must always be secondary to just economic structures, safe working conditions, and adequate housing for vulnerable persons.

With what shall I come before the LORD,
and bow myself before God on high?
Shall I come before him with burnt offerings,
with calves a year old?

> *Will the LORD be pleased with thousands of rams,*
> *with ten thousands of rivers of oil?*
> *Shall I give my firstborn for my transgression,*
> *the fruit of my body for the sin of my soul?"*
> *He has told you, O mortal, what is good;*
> *and what does the LORD require of you*
> *but to do justice, and to love kindness,*
> *and to walk humbly with your God. (Micah 6:6–8)*

A PASSIONATE SPIRITUALITY

Jesus incarnates the divine quest for justice. He was a child of the prophets, and he embodied the prophetic vision in his care for the outcast, sick, and strangers. His radical hospitality embraced every spectrum of human experience and every social station. Jesus's healing ministry was a reflection of his prophetic faith; his embrace of the untouchable and unclean as well as the Roman oppressor broke down barriers of "in" and "out." Jesus himself became ritually unclean to secure the well-being of his culture's most maligned and vulnerable persons.

His pain over injustice and exclusion reveal the radical vision of God as truly one with us, feeling our pain, delighting at our joy, and being touched intimately by our actions. Jesus revealed divine perfection as passionate and caring, and divine uniqueness as ever-flowing loving-kindness and intimacy. In contrast to Aristotle's vision of divinity as unchanging and untouched by the imperfections of mortality—the emotionally "unmoved mover"—Jesus reveals God as the "most moved mover," touching and being touched by all things and dynamically moving within history to inspire us to justice and Earth-care.

Listen to these words from Jesus's inaugural sermon (Luke 4:18–19) in the spirit of lectio divina. *Take a moment to experience a facet of God's vision for us individually and corporately as you contemplate this passage from the Gospel that quotes Hebraic scriptures. If you believed these words and lived by them, how would they change your life? What words of guidance, challenge, and consolation do they give you?*

The Spirit of God is upon me, because God has anointed me to bring good news to the poor. God has sent me to proclaim release to the captives and recovery of sight to the blind, to let the oppressed go free, to proclaim the year of God's favor.

Jesus's first followers lived this vision by creating communities in which personal property was considered communal; that is, at the disposal of the community's need and the needs of its most vulnerable members. Within the body of Christ, overall health depended on the well-being of each member, especially its most vulnerable members. While the practices of the Jesus's first followers do not provide a blueprint for public policy, they invite us to imagine a society in which people's needs and well-being are placed above profit. How we use our property is a spiritual issue insofar as all good gifts come from our Loving Parent. Our largesse is not our own but intended to support the well-being of others.

Nothing is further from Jesus's viewpoint than the individualistic, self-made individual, accountable only to self-interest, exalted in the work of Ayn Rand and her followers. Our most vulnerable companions matter in economics and public policy because we are all connected as members of the body of Christ. Our joys and sorrows are one, and our just actions promote our wholeness as well as the wholeness of others. Scripture challenges us to fill our spirits so that others might experience the Spirit more fully. Christ calls us to consume wisely, so that the birds of the air, the lilies of the field, and innocent children might realize God's dream for them.

> *They devoted themselves to the apostles' teaching and fellowship, to the breaking of bread and the prayers. Awe came upon everyone, because many wonders and signs were being done by the apostles. All who believed were together and had all things in common; they would sell their possessions and goods and distribute the proceeds to all, as any had need. Day by day, as they spent much time together in the*

temple, they broke bread at home and at their food with glad and generous hearts, praising God and having the goodwill of the people. And day by day God added to their number those who were being saved. (Acts 2:42–47)

In the body of Christ, and ultimately in the world, what happens to one eventually shapes everyone else. If one part of the body rejoices, all rejoice; if one part of the body suffers, all suffer. Accordingly, the goal of Christian community is to create healthy human villages (or churches) made up of healthy members, nurtured by healthy behaviors. These healthy congregations are lights to the world, contributing to the health of the communities around them.

What we do matters to our neighbor and it also matters to God. Our calling, as Mother Teresa affirmed, is to do something beautiful for God, for as we have done to the least of these, the most vulnerable, we have done to God (Matthew 25:34–40). Our lives are our gifts to God; what we do truly makes a difference to God and is experienced positively or negatively, promoting life or death, in persons and the environment. God is the fellow sufferer who understands our struggles and the joyful companion who celebrates our well-being.

No doubt, Jesus was familiar with the words of the Hebraic prophets Amos and Hosea whose ministry was motivated by the following affirmations: "Let justice roll down like waters and righteousness like an ever-flowing stream" (Amos 5:24). "What does God require of you—to do justice, to love kindness, and to walk humbly with your God" (Micah 6:8).

The prophetic witness of Jesus and his earliest followers relates to the whole person in that individual's concrete environment. Love takes shape in how we treat one another, especially in acts of mercy and affirmation that bring healing to the world. As the bumper sticker states: "If you love Jesus, seek justice; any fool can honk!"

God is present in every situation; God comes to us, providing us with inspiration, nurture, and challenge in each moment and encounter. Our spiritual stature comes from the compassionate quest for a world in which every person might experience happiness, abundance, and growth. In the quest for social healing, prayer and meditation are not optional; they awaken us to the unity of all creation and the intricate and dynamic fabric of relatedness from which every life emerges.

SPIRITUAL OPENINGS

This spiritual practice enables us to experience the essential unity of life and our connection with all creation.

Begin with stillness and gentle breathing. After you have found your quiet center, visualize your closest friends and relatives, feeling your deep connection with them. In your imagination, begin to experience Christ's face as you look upon each one of them. Feel their joy and pain, and their need of healing.

Now expand your attention to visualize strangers in their joy and sorrow, seeing Christ's face as you gaze upon them. Further expanding on your connection with the world around you, visualize Christ's face as you look upon people from other countries, even countries that consider your country as an adversary. Take time to visualize their joy and pain, and your common humanity.

Going beyond the human community, experience the holiness of the nonhuman world: birds, fireflies, sea otters, polar bears, whales, and all plant and animal life. Feel your connection with the flow of all creation as beloved by God and revealing divine wisdom.

Conclude with a time of gratitude for the wondrous interdependence of life and your own vocation to be God's partner in healing the Earth.

ELEVEN

SPIRITUALITY FOR ALL THE SEASONS OF LIFE

My God, my God, why have you forsaken me?
Why are you so far from helping me,
from the words of my groaning?
O my God, I cry by day but you do not answer;
And by night, but find no rest.

Psalm 22:1–2

Even though I walk through the darkest valley,
I fear no evil; For you are with me,
your rod and your staff—they comfort me....
Surely goodness and mercy shall follow me
all the days of my life, and I shall dwell
in the house of God all my life long.

Psalm 23:4, 6

Life is suffering,
but we can find release from suffering.

The First and Third of Gautama the Buddha's
Four Noble Truths, adapted

PRAYING THE PSALMS

Episcopalian spiritual leader Alan Jones notes that spirituality deals with the unfixable realities of life, those necessary occurrences that we can neither evade nor ignore but must confront and transform. A complete life contains moments of celebration and desolation, of affirmation and abandonment, of gratitude and doubt. As the author of Ecclesiastes counsels, there is a time for every season under heaven.

In this chapter, we will be praying the Psalms as a pathway of spiritual growth. The Psalms confront life in all its dimensions. They are unvarnished in their portrayal of the human condition. The Psalms address every situation of life: in them, we observe praise and challenge, intimacy and absence, and reconciliation and violence. Their message is that God is at work in every season of life and that we can bring the totality of our lives, without exception, to God. God feels our pain and joy and our elation and depression, and embraces us unconditionally, loving us when we are most unlovable and comforting us when we've lost everything. The Psalms invite us to dialogue with the Hindu vision of spiritual pathways for every season of life—youth, marriage and young adulthood, midlife, retirement, aging, and preparation for death. Every season of life has its own particular vocations and can be seen as an opportunity to encounter the divine.

PRAYING WITH CREATION

The Psalms celebrate a wild and enchanted universe. All nature bursts forth in praise and reveals divine wisdom. We are not alone in the universe; we are part of a living, breathing, evolving, and interdependent reality. The universe is wonderful and wild beyond our wildest imaginings (Psalm 148–150). The authors of this ancient poetry would have been filled with awe at photographs from the Hubble Telescope and would have praised God for the complexity of fetal life (Psalm 139) as well as the immensity of the universe (Psalm 8). We live in a glorious universe, whose grandeur and beauty can never be erased by human misuse. We find our place in the universe by breathing along with all creation. Joined with all creatures, we discover our vocation as partners in praise with babbling brooks, flickering fireflies, soaring eagles, and dancing dolphins.

Pause awhile right now and look around, even if you are in an office suite or far away from anything you consider arboreal: What beauty do you notice? What realities make your life possible? What is your relationship with the ambient universe?

Perhaps, as the philosopher Alfred North Whitehead proclaims, the whole universe is at work in the emergence of every new moment of experience. The whole universe flows in and through you, filling you with its constantly creating energy.

Take a moment to contemplate creation. Feel, as you breathe, the rhythms of life moving through you and energizing you. Begin by quietly reflecting on the words of Psalm 150:6: "Let everything that breathes, praise God." In the silence, breathe deeply and slowly. Experience each breath as divine inspiration, moving through your life and all creation—and as an invitation to connect with the wider world. Sense your connection with God's presence in every creature, most especially the nonhuman world. Feel the holy energy of the Big Bang and 14 billion years of cosmic evolution flowing through you. Give thanks for your connection with God and all of life. As you experience your relationship with your companions on this planet, with whom you are joined in the wondrous ecology of spirit and flesh, feel the energy of creation moving in and around and through you, giving birth to every cell in your body.

Conclude by affirming the beauty of creation and making a commitment to love God from whom all blessings flow within the created realm.

When we face the seasons of life with a sense of radical amazement and gratitude, we are able to embrace the unwanted and unfixable moments of pain and defeat. All of life finds its meaning in relationship to the One whose love embraces every dimension of human experience.

MOVEMENTS OF THE SPIRIT

Bible scholar Walter Brueggemann describes three movements in the personal and communal spirituality of the Psalms:

Orientation: A sense of contentment and gratitude for the goodness of life, the order of the universe, and the blessings we experience as persons and as a community.

Disorientation: The experience of life falling apart, punctuated by the apparent absence of God. In despair, we cry out: Why has God forsaken us? Why am I alone in the universe? How long can I endure this pain?

New orientation: The experience of healing and new creation within and beyond life's troubles. New life emerges out of the rubble and we have a renewed sense of divine intimacy and goodness despite the challenges of life. As we go through the darkest night, we discover God's protective and guiding presence. While we can never go back to the way things were, we can experience healing and transformation that places pain, failure, and absence within the wider perspective of God's tender mercies.[21]

The broad vision of the Psalms invites us to a spirituality of stature. Healthy spirituality joins us with creation in all its beauty, wonder, and surprise. It also connects deeply with our pain and the suffering of others. Spiritual maturity sensitizes us to the pain of others and awakens us to life in all its tragic beauty.

WONDER-FILLED SPIRITUALITY

Prayerfully read Psalm 8 as a psalm of celebration and wonder. What insight does the psalm suggest about the relationship of God and humankind? How might it shape our understanding of our vocation as created in God's image?

O LORD, our Sovereign,
how majestic is your name in all the earth!
You have set your glory above the heavens.
Out of the mouths of babes and infants
you have founded a bulwark because of your foes,
to silence the enemy and the avenger.
When I look at your heavens, the work of your fingers,
the moon and the stars that you have established;
what are human beings that you are mindful of them,
mortals that you care for them?
Yet you have made them a little lower than God,
and crowned them with glory and honor.
You have given them dominion
over the works of your hands;
you have put all things under their feet,
all sheep and oxen, and also the beasts of the field,

> *the birds of the air, and the fish of the sea,*
> *whatever passes along the paths of the seas.*
> *O LORD, our Sovereign,*
> *how majestic is your name in all the earth!*

The composer of Psalm 8 would rejoice in today's scientific vision of an immense universe, infinite in space and time. Unlike today's Christian proponents of a "young Earth" less than ten thousand years old, the psalmist would have appreciated the Hindu vision of a multi-billion-year, multi-galactic universe. The psalmist is overcome with radical amazement at the grandeur of the universe; his imagination is stretched to its limits. We can imagine him writing, were he alive today: "Who are we humans and our planet amid the 125 billion galaxies, each galaxy with a billion stars like our sun? What is the significance of our moment of time in the fourteen-billion-year evolutionary journey? Do we matter at all?"

Despite our mortality and finitude, the psalmist shouts, "Yes!" God is here in our world and lives; the Great Soul of the Universe (Brahman) also moves within our localized spiritual lives (Atman). If God is present everywhere, then God is also present in the brevity and limitations of lives and in the evolution and destiny of our little blue and green planet. We are centered in God and so is everything else. We matter and we have a place that is unique and irreplaceable in God's vision of reality. Indeed, connected with God, we are joined with all things in God's everlasting adventure.

We have, the psalmist realizes, a home in the universe, centered right here on Earth, and our vocation is to be God's companions in caring for the planet. We are responsible for nurturing the Earth and its inhabitants, furthering the creative adventure that God imagines for humankind and God's good Earth.

Jewish spiritual teacher Abraham Joshua Heschel has asserted that radical amazement is at the heart of the spiritual journey. If your spirituality doesn't inspire awe at the heavens above and the Earth around us, at the movements of galaxies and our immune and nervous systems, it is unlikely that it will be of any use in responding to the critical economic, ecological, and political issues of our time. Feelings of radical amazement deepen our appreciation of everyday life. Studies indicate that mystical, awe-filled experiences enhance feelings of altruism and compassion. Having experienced our intimate connection with life in all its forms, our calling is to heal the world one person and one planet at a time.

A SPIRITUALITY THAT GRIEVES AND LAMENTS

Dynamic spirituality embraces the totality of human experience. Part of the wonder of life is found in its fragility. Recognizing our mortality awakens us to the preciousness of each moment in its grandeur and tragedy. "In the midst of life, we are surrounded by death,"

Martin Luther noted. With illness and death come the threat of isolation, pain, loneliness, and grief. Grief over the loss of loved ones, as well as the loss of physical stamina and mental acuity, eventually touches us all and those we love. As the Serenity Prayer suggests, some things can't be fixed or changed—but they can be transformed. Still, we can find a higher power in the deepest darkness.

Dark moods, brought on by feelings of grief and abandonment, characterize the lamentations of Psalm 22. Listen deeply to the words of this psalm. Have you felt this way? Have you ever felt the absence of God? How did you survive it? How did you rediscover God's presence?

My God, my God, why have you forsaken me?
Why are you so far from helping me,
from the words of my groaning?
O my God, I cry by day, but you do not answer;
and by night, but find no rest.
Yet you are holy, enthroned on the praises of Israel.
In you our ancestors trusted;
they trusted, and you delivered them.
To you they cried, and were saved;
in you they trusted, and were not put to shame.

> *But I am a worm, and not human;*
> *scorned by others, and despised by the people.*
> *All who see me mock at me;*
> *they make mouths at me, they shake their heads;*
> *"Commit your cause to the LORD; let him deliver—*
> *let him rescue the one in whom he delights!"*
> *…Do not be far from me, for trouble is near*
> *and there is no one to help.* (Psalm 22:1–8, 11)

These are harsh and dreadful words. There is anger and hopelessness in them. Surprisingly, they are addressed to God, the psalmist's apparently absent parent. Despite his sense of divine neglect, the psalmist cries out to God—and so do we—hoping for more than silence, knowing we have nowhere else to turn. Will God hear our prayers? Will we discover life in the midst of death?

Life remains brutal and we feel abandoned, but in crying out to the God we perceive as absent, we—like the psalmist—discover God's presence, faint and obscure, yet hovering within the jagged edges of life, providing enough hope for us to endure today's trials and take the next step to recovery.

PRESENCE IN DARKNESS

No doubt, the placement of Psalm 22 and 23 is not accidental but speaks to the many seasons of faith: sorrow and joy, abandonment and celebration, distance and presence. Psalm 23, the "Shepherd Psalm," is one of the best-known and most-loved passages in scripture, invoked in times of personal and communal mourning, often punctuating funeral and graveside services. Let us meditate on these words with new ears, opening to our pain and God's presence.

Pause a moment to breathe deeply, awakening to God's presence with every breath. Place your life in God's care, one breath at a time. Open to the wisdom of these words of scripture.

> *The LORD is my shepherd, I shall not want.*
> *He makes me lie down in green pastures;*
> *he leads me beside still waters; he restores my soul.*
> *He leads me in right paths for his name's sake.*
> *Even though I walk through the darkest valley,*
> *I fear no evil; for you are with me;*
> *your rod and your staff—they comfort me.*
> *You prepare a table before me*
> *in the presence of my enemies;*
> *you anoint my head with oil; my cup overflows.*
> *Surely goodness and mercy shall follow me*
> *all the days of my life, and I shall dwell*
> *in the house of the LORD my whole life long*

What feelings does this psalm evoke? Are you able to experience God's nearness amid your current challenges and feelings of fear and anxiety? What would it mean to overflow with love in the midst of conflict?

This is truly an all-season psalm. There is no denial here. Celebration comes in the midst of threat. Divine protection acknowledges that there are enemies waiting to threaten our physical, spiritual, emotional, and mental well-being. The psalmist has been to hell, touched rock bottom, and discovered that while faith does not insulate us from life's trials, God is as much present in danger and disease as in comfort and health. Enemies lurk in the darkness outside the warmth and light of the tent, but we can feast on the goodness of life, knowing that God is with us, caring for us "where the wild things are." Ultimately we can't go around the valley—we must go through it—but we are never alone.

As I write these words, two close friends are in the midst of chemotherapy treatments. In the case of one, this is the third recurrence of what is described as "incurable" colon cancer. Neither of them can deny the threat of death and the painful side effects of the treatments intended to restore them, at least temporarily in the case of one, to health. Both are learning to find God in the midst of their treatments and to experience them as sacramental gifts of God, reflecting God's aim at healing and wholeness. Darkness surrounds their paths, but they are discovering the unfailing love of God is with them, even in the darkness. Both are learning to live by the Apostle Paul's affirmation, most likely written from prison: "Whether we live or die, we belong to God" (Romans 14:8).

This spring, a dear congregant passed away. When she decided to discontinue chemotherapy, she knew that her days were numbered. She faced the final months of her life, trusting the love of friends and the nearness of God, whom she believed would receive her with loving arms at the hour of her death.

EMBRACING OUR WHOLE SELVES

Spiritual transformation embraces the whole person, including our bodies and emotions. The healing of emotions comes from accepting them fully—both positive and negative feelings—in light of God's graceful care.

Many persons involved in contemporary spiritual movements deny negativity in all its dimensions. They counsel us to tamp down our anger and anxiety, accentuate the positive, and eliminate the negative. They judge persons who become angry at injustice or personal affronts as spiritually immature and suggest that their emotions may be the primary source of disease and misfortune.

Although healthy spirituality invites us to affirm God's abundant life and our essential wholeness as God's beloved children, I believe we also need to address feelings of anger, shame, fear, anxiety, and negativity.

The traditional practice of confession is intended to promote mindfulness and bring healing to our conscious and unconscious minds. What isn't noticed and accepted will often be projected on others in the form of negative comments, scapegoating, passive-aggressive behavior, polarization, and violence. As Richard Rohr sagely notes, "If you don't transform the pain, you will always transmit it."[22] Honoring the whole of our experience enables us to appreciate and accept our own imperfections and the imperfections of others, even when we need to challenge and amend certain behaviors and actions. Spaciousness and spiritual stature are the fruits of embracing our whole lives in their beauty and brokenness.

The words of Psalm 139, described earlier in this book, capture the holistic spirituality of the entire Book of Psalms, and they bear repeating here. This psalm expresses the grandest and vilest of human sentiments. It invites us to recognize and then present our greatness and pettiness as materials for God's transformation of our lives. The Divine Artist always seeks to redeem the wreckage of our lives. God brings forth tragic beauty from the joys and sorrows of our world. In a spirit of confessional acceptance, listen with your whole self to these words from Psalm 139:

O LORD, you have searched me and known me.
You know when I sit down and when I rise up;
you discern my thoughts from far away.

You search out my path and my lying down,
and are acquainted with all my ways.
Even before a word is on my tongue,
O LORD, you know it completely.
You hem me in, behind and before,
and lay your hand upon me.
Such knowledge is too wonderful for me;
it is so high that I cannot attain it.
Where can I go from your spirit?
Or where can I flee from your presence?
If I ascend to heaven, you are there;
if I make my bed in Sheol, you are there.
If I take the wings of the morning
and settle at the farthest limits of the sea,
even there your hand shall lead me,
and your right hand shall hold me fast.
If I say, "Surely the darkness shall cover me,
and the light around me become night,"
even the darkness is not dark to you;
the night is as bright as the day,
for darkness is as light to you….
O that you would kill the wicked, O God,
and that the bloodthirsty would depart from me—

> *those who speak of you maliciously,*
> *and lift themselves up against you for evil!*
> *Do I not hate those who hate you, O LORD?*
> *And do I not loathe those who rise up against you?*
> *I hate them with perfect hatred;*
> *I count them my enemies.*
> *Search me, O God, and know my heart;*
> *test me and know my thoughts.*
> *See if there is any wicked way in me,*
> *and lead me in the way everlasting.*

Do you notice the change in tone? The psalm moves from wonder at God's intimacy and presence in every life situation to words of hatred and violence. But then, as if in recognition of his inner turmoil and temptation to annihilate his enemies, the psalmist pauses and asks God once more to "search and know" his heart and examine his conscience with hope that he may be emotionally and spiritually healed. Psalm 139 reminds us that in the heights and depths of life, in moments of mysticism and mayhem, God's care guides, surrounds, and transforms us. As the Apostle Paul said centuries later, "Nothing can separate us from the love of God," not even our deepest temptations and most shameful feelings.

Psalm 139, in its embrace of the totality of our experience, is an example of spiritual mindfulness, similar to that taught by Vietnamese Buddhist monk Thich Nhat Hanh or North American mindfulness meditation teacher John Kabat-Zinn. Listening to the whole of our lives, we discover the holiness of each moment, even moments of illness and imperfection.

The Psalms testify to God's loving presence in every moment of life. As Ecclesiastes witnesses, "For everything there is a season"; and in all the seasons of life—abundance and scarcity, health and illness, wealth and poverty, calm and anxiety, youth and age—God is near. God has the final word over every life, and that word is "yes." In the spirit of a grace that will never abandon us and always affirm us, we can sing the last line of the Psalms, "Let everything that breathes praise God."

In creatively responding to the seasons of life, let us consider a traditional Jewish spiritual practice based on the Psalms, "the complete remedy," or the *Tikkun HaKlali*. Rabbi Nachman of Beslov (1772–1810), the grandson of the Baal Shem Tov (the Master of a Good Name), the founder of Hasidic Judaism, asserted that reciting ten psalms daily can bring forgiveness of sin, healing of the spirit, and personal transformation. In the intricate interdependence of mind, body, and spirit, they may even improve your physical well-being. While Rabbi Nachman counseled reciting these healing psalms an hour daily, we may profit from slowly reading each psalm with a moment in between. The psalms that Rabbi Nachman recommended for spiritual transformation are: 16, 32, 41, 42, 59, 77, 90, 105, 137, 150. In the spirit of Buddhist bodhisattvas, Nachman promised: "When my days are over and I leave this world, I will still intercede for anyone who comes to my grave, says these Ten Psalms, and gives a penny to charity. No matter how great his sins, I will do everything in my power, spanning the length and breadth of creation, to save and cleanse that person."[23]

SPIRITUAL OPENINGS

Take a few days to recite the Ten Psalms, listed above, in order, opening in the process to God's transforming love. Let go of the past and awaken to God's constantly replenishing energy of love and new life. Begin this time of reflection with a moment of stillness, experiencing God's companionship and affirmation. After reading each psalm, breathe deeply the healing winds of grace with confidence that the One who searches and knows also accepts and transforms. The Divine Artist makes all things new and uses even our faults and negative experiences as materials for new creation.

Reciting the Psalms may awaken a sense of divine forgiveness, protection, gratitude, healing, intimacy, and hunger for wholeness. As you breathe these psalms in the spirit of the final words of the Tenth Healing Psalm, Psalm 150, you may discover God breathing in and through you, connecting you in a holy way with every creature. Let everything that breathes, praise God!

TWELVE

WALKING IN HOLINESS AND WONDER

Solvitur ambulando!
It will be solved in the walking.

Augustine of Hippo

With beauty all around me, I walk.

Navajo Blessing Way

Peace is every step.
This shining sun is in my heart.
Each flower smiles with me.
How green, how fresh is all that grows.
How cool the wind blows.
Peace is every step.
It turns the endless path to joy.[24]

Buddhist spiritual teacher, Thich Nhat Hanh

SOLVED IN THE WALKING

I love to walk. On a good day, I take the two-mile walk from my Cape Cod congregation to the edge of the Craigville Retreat Center and back to church once in the morning and again in the afternoon or evening. When I travel on holiday or to give talks, retreats, or workshops, I make it a point to bring my walking shoes and hit the road before daylight to ground myself in God's presence and experience the reality that wherever I am, I am home.

The first Christians described themselves as the people of the Way. The lived out their faith as they walked on the pathways of the Risen Jesus, sharing healing and God's good news along the way. Doctrine and institution were secondary and could be adapted to the pathways they traveled. Centuries later, Celtic Christians drew circles around themselves in prayer as they began each journey, whether it be to the market or on a mission, knowing that each step forward was an adventure, filled with both possibility and threat. As important as yesterday's traditions are, we must remember that we discover their meaning for today as we too take each new step, making up our own faith journeys in partnership as we walk along. A walking faith reminds us that God is known in the walking.

The ancient couple, Adam and Eve, whose mythical journey of sin and grace is repeated in every life, came to their senses and experienced their alienation from their Creator when "they heard the sound of God walking in the garden at the time of the evening breeze" (Genesis 3:8). Even God goes for a walk! The anthropomorphic vision of God described in the Genesis story points to the deep reality that the Holy One is on the move, creating, revealing, and healing.

Wherever we go, God is with us, however circuitous our journeys may be. Even when we run away from God, we discover that God is already waiting with open arms. As *The Runaway Bunny*, the children's book by Margaret Wise Brown, portrays, God (like the mother rabbit) will run alongside us, taking whatever form is necessary to remind us that nothing can separate us from Divine Love. Along the road to Emmaus, two dejected walkers encounter a stranger who walks beside them, sharing conversation, until he is revealed as the Risen Jesus in the breaking of the bread. God is not on the throne; God is on the move. God is not far off, immune from life's pain and joy; God is with us, right beside us. In the words of the hymn I learned in my small-town Baptist church:

> *And he walks with me,*
> *And he talks with me,*
> *And he tells me I am his own,*
> *And the joy we share*
> *As we tarry there,*
> *None other has ever known.*[25]

Spiritual transformation is about movement, embodiment, and awakening to holiness with every step. As Thich Nhat Hanh proclaims, peace is every step!

THE LABYRINTH OF LOVE

A church in downtown Washington, DC, announces on its marquee, "Where all are pilgrims and none are strangers." This could be the theme for this text. We are all pilgrims and adventurers even if we never leave home. Every day is filled with adventures, possibilities, and challenges. Spiritual growth comes from embracing transformation and experiencing God's ever-evolving vision. The quest for our quiet center awakens us to a gentle providence, always enveloping, healing, and moving forward. While God's love and companionship—God's aim at abundant life—is unchanging, God's vision is constantly evolving and inviting us to evolve with it. The waves of divine love are as real as the calm of ocean depths.

Today, many persons are rediscovering their spiritual centers through movement by walking a sacred labyrinth. Not a maze to confuse but a spiritual path to inspire, the labyrinth reveals the truth that while we may walk the same path each day, with each step we can become a new creation. The labyrinth testifies to the truth that the journey inward and outward are one and the same, and that spiritual growth involves moving through the valleys of joy and sorrow, accepting each day's challenges.

Lauren Artress, whose *Walking a Sacred Path* awakened interest in the labyrinth as a spiritual tool, asserts that the labyrinth is "a container for the creative imagination to align with our heart's desire, it is a place where we can profoundly, yet playfully express our soul's longing and intention."[26] The labyrinth is a moveable "thin place" where divine inspiration and human intuition meet. In walking the labyrinth, we are pilgrims in motion attuning ourselves to the divine movements toward wholeness in our lives.

There are many ways to walk a sacred path: you may come to the labyrinth with a question, a quest for guidance, a search for truth, or a simple openness to whatever surfaces. You can walk slowly, taking a breath with each step, or skip along the turning pathway. You may choose to meditate at the labyrinth's center or continue on your path outward without stopping. In walking this sacred path, we let go of control and move in accordance with the insights we receive along the way. Whether at Chartres or the National Cathedral in Washington, DC, or in the garden of a local congregation, labyrinths are archetypes of our lifelong pilgrim path.

Paul Tillich once suggested that we participate in the Lord's Supper so that every meal might become holy. We walk the labyrinth for the same reason: to discover and affirm the holiness of every step we take. Wisdom, insight, inspiration, intuition, and synchronicity are available at every turn. Healing can be found in every encounter. Burning bushes lie on every pathway. The labyrinth awakens us to the nearness of God in every life situation.

A wise spiritual guide once counseled, "Pray as you can and not as you can't." The same wisdom applies to walking the labyrinth. Let the Spirit lure you forward and guide your pace as you open to your own creative wisdom, as well as God's creativity moving within you. Let the wisdom of the unconscious, the home of spiritual symbols and divine inspiration, come to you in sighs too deep for words and guide your steps within and beyond the labyrinth.

JUST A CLOSER WALK

In the course of writing these meditations, I have sought to embrace the totality of my spiritual journey from my Baptist routes, though psychedelic adventures, Hindu and Buddhist studies, the healings of Jesus and global healing, Christian mysticism, and the evolving wisdom of global and integrative Christianity. I have recalled encounters on my own holy adventure that I had long forgotten and have bathed myself in memories of camping in Big Sur; going to a Transcendental Meditation New Year's retreat in Asilomar, California; dancing with Hare Krishna devotees in a parade in San Francisco; and singing hymns in my Baptist church in King City, California. As I pondered a walking spirituality, I recalled the refrain of another childhood hymn I learned at my Salinas Valley childhood church:

> *Just a closer walk with Thee,*
> *Grant it, Jesus, is my plea,*
> *Daily walking close to Thee,*

Let it be, dear Lord, let it be.[27]

This hymn is still my prayer. Although the Jesus with whom I walk is now much bigger than my childhood Christianity and untrammeled by the narrow pathways of some doctrines or institutions, I still want to walk with Jesus on my pilgrim pathway. I need guidance step by step to navigate each day as well as the long haul of life. Aligned with the mind of Christ, I will find my way and discover a wise companion who walks alongside me, guiding every step. And so I walk on!

BEAUTY ALL AROUND

Thornton Wilder's play *Our Town* has a scene in which Emily asks to come back from the dead to relive one day of her life. She is overwhelmed with emotion and asks her spectral companions, "Does anyone ever realize life while they life it...every, every minute?" The stage manager, speaking from a God's-eye view, responds that such a gift may only come to saints and poets. Emily laments her failure to experience the fullness of life: "Oh, earth, you're too wonderful for anyone to realize you." William Blake captured this same vision in his recognition that "if the doors of perception were cleansed, everything would appear as it is, infinite."

Wilder and Blake capture the mystic's vision. God is present in all things and all things reveal divinity. I find that walking opens up my personal doors of perception, calms my spirit, awakens my energy centers, and fills my senses with beauty and wonder. Sometimes as I walk, I simply let my senses wander with no particular agenda. I experience holy wisdom and wonder in scudding clouds, the feel of raindrops and wind on my cheeks, the sound of wild geese honking, the view of a sliver moon and distant stars, or the flashing of summer fireflies. I don't plan for such experiences or practice a complicated spiritual discipline; I am simply aware, all sense and intuition, of letting Life flow in and through me. Yet perhaps there is an intention in this effortless nonintentionality—the intention of experiencing with mindful appreciation this present moment in all its temporariness and wonder. In such moments, I feel like a cell in the body of God, experiencing the world as God experiences it and opening to God experiencing the world through me.

There are other times when we choose to be intentional about our peripatetic spiritual practices. As we saunter along, we need to take time to reflect on the day's events, pause to sit on a bench or rock, and to pray our deepest needs. We also need in such intentional times to leave room for spontaneous encounters with divine serendipity. This is the vision of Wordsworth's child "trailing crowds of glory." It is the summer day in which Mary Oliver experiences eternity as she merges her spirit with a grasshopper chewing a blade of grass. It is Manhattan in all its glory, seen as a manifestation of the many-faceted God experienced by the meandering Walt Whitman. It is Isaiah in the Temple experiencing the whole Earth filled with God's glory. Surely, with beauty all around us, we walk.

SPIRITUAL OPENINGS

Solvitur ambulando! It will be solved in the walking! Walking in beauty in this present moment is miraculous enough. Still, intentionality opens us to the infinite movement of life that flows in and through us. We can encounter the holy through both slow and aerobic prayer walking.

Begin with the intention to listen for divine wisdom with your whole being as you move slowly and steadily. Start walking slowly and contemplatively, immersing yourself in this Holy Here-and-Now with each step. With each step, slow your pace. Eventually, take a step every few seconds. Pay attention to your breath, your body, your heart, and your mind. You might invoke the words of Buddhist spiritual guide Thich Nhat Hanh:

> *Breathing in,*
>
> *I feel calm.*
>
> *Breathing out,*
>
> *I smile.*[28]

Whenever you become distracted, focus on the feeling of your feet contacting the ground with each step. Conclude this contemplative time with thanksgiving for the opportunity to connect more fully with the divine.

Take some time to reflect on your experience of slow walking prayer.

Here is an aerobic walking prayer, similar to the practice I follow. My practice is truly interspiritual as it joins the wisdom of East and West, of Jesus's companionship and Hindu and Chinese understandings of the chakra system and universal (ki) energy. You may adapt this in ways that suit your theology, spirituality, or walking style. I walk at a pace of about 3.3 miles an hour as I practice this prayer form.

Begin with some deep breaths. Either silently or by making a spoken affirmation such as "This is the day that God has made and I will rejoice and be glad in it," begin walking at your normal pace or a comfortable aerobic pace. As you breathe in the beauty of the world around you—and cities and bustling walkways can be beautiful, too!—experience God's calming and healing energy flowing in and through you. Gently experience the divine energy flowing in and through your crown (the top of your head), forehead, throat, chest and lungs, solar plexus, genitals, and anus (root). Feel each of these energy centers opening and balancing with each breath. Take a moment or two to breathe through each energy center, feeling revived and energized. As you come to the anus or root chakra, take a few extra breaths. Now take a few moments as you lift up a few people in prayer. Experience them centered and surrounded by divine healing light. Return to the crown, breathing God's light in and through each center of energy. On the upward way, take a moment to repeat affirmations at each energy center as you experience God's energy flow in and out. Here are some possible affirmations:

>**Root:** *I let go of the past and open to divine creativity.*
>**Genitals:** *Divine energy and creativity flow in and through me.*
>**Solar plexus:** *I experience divine vitality in every cell of my body and every feeling and thought.*
>**Chest/heart:** *Nothing can separate me from the love of God.*
>**Neck:** *The words I speak bring healing to everyone I meet.*
>**Forehead:** *Divine intelligence guides every decision I make.*
>**Crown:** *I am constantly inspired and act in accordance with divine wisdom.*

Conclude your walk, whether it is ten minutes or an hour, with a time of thanksgiving, petition, and intercession.

THIRTEEN

REJOICING IN MULTIPLICITY

*In my Parent's house,
there are many dwelling places.*

John 14:2

*Now there are a variety of gifts but the same Spirit;
and there are varieties of services,
but the same Lord;
and there are varieties of activities,
but it is the same God
who activates all of them in everyone.*

1 Corinthians 12:4–6

GOD'S GLORIOUS DIVERSITY

It has been said that variety is the spice of life. I believe that variety is also the spice of spiritual transformation and divine revelation. Often people view Christianity and other world religions as static, monolithic, and uniform in practice and doctrine. Nothing could be further from the truth. When someone claims to be an "orthodox" Christian, I often retort, "Which orthodoxy are you talking about—the orthodoxy of the Apostles and Nicene Creeds, pre-eleventh century Western Christianity, Eastern Orthodoxy, Reformation Protestant, Calvinism, Anabaptism, Anglican, or Wesleyan?" The same is true for virtually every other faith tradition. Just think about the difference between Shin Buddhism's devotional piety and trust in Amida's saving grace and the quiet self-reliance of Zen Buddhism or the Buddha's earliest teachings—or the differences among Shi'ite, Sunni, and Sufi forms of Islam. Hindus recognize a variety of yogas, each of which responds to certain personality types or spiritual orientations. As H. Richard Niebuhr noted several decades ago, revelation always requires a receiver whose social and historical location and experience always shapes the character of the community's revelatory experiences.

Microcosm and macrocosm mirror each other. Variety is also inherent in the creative process. Our world is populated by an amazing array of galaxies, species, and colors. In the ongoing evolution of life, new species, solar systems, and galaxies continue to emerge. The evolutionary process, embodied in human and nonhuman life, never takes a holiday from birth, death, growth, and transformation.

Variety is essential to the spiritual landscape. While some people believe that spiritual diversity is a fall from grace and a sign of humanity's turning from God, an alternative explanation is that God shapes the divine encounter with humankind according to location, personality, geography, culture, and history. God always speaks to people in the concrete, not as abstractions or in terms of cookie-cutter sameness. Desert people describe the Holy One in ways quite different from mountain, river, and ocean peoples. In the call-and-response of revelation and receiver, a Buddha could only have emerged from the Hindu tradition, an Isaiah only out of the Hebraic tradition, and a Mohammed only from the Jewish and Christian traditions. Even the teachings and healing practices of Jesus had historical and cultural precedents. Jesus's unique revelation of God emerged in dialogue with the historically oriented, body-affirming, and politically conscious traditions of the prophets, wisdom teachers, and children of Israel.

Christian theology affirms the diversity inherent in the divine nature. The Holy Trinity is wholly one and wholly many. The dance of the Trinity (perichoresis) parents varieties of revelations, just as divine creativity parents countless species of plants and animals in a universe of countless galaxies and solar systems.

PRISMATIC SPIRITUALITY

This book is a testimony to what philosopher-psychologist William James described as the "varieties of religious experience" and the multiplicity of spiritual practices and experiences. Spirituality is intimate and polyvalent in nature, with as many possible revelations as there are Divine-human encounters, cultural expressions, and sides to God. In contrast to unchanging, uniform, and homogenous visions of God, I believe that the ever-faithful God is also ever-changing, complex, and multifaceted in expression and action.

Our various experiences of God may be described in terms of the movements of the sun streaming through an ever-moving prism. Prior to Copernicus and the discoveries of modern astronomy, spiritual and scientific teachers would have felt justified in describing the sun as eternal and immobile. Today, we know different: the sun itself is alive and in constant motion, moving on its own axis, sending forth flares, and manifesting firestorms. Fluid and vital, the sun energizes and inspires the changing hues emanating from a prism that is itself in motion.

God is always—as the apophatic tradition asserts—beyond description. As Hindu philosophy affirms, we can never fathom the fullness of divinity in its consciousness, bliss, and becoming. God is also—as the kataphatic tradition indicates—the fullness of becoming, dynamically manifesting divine creativity in myriad and evolving ways. This is good news for the spiritual seeker: God comes to us in a multitude of ways. We can find divinity in the seasons of the Earth; in the child Jesus in the manger, the Galilean teacher and healer, and the man on the Cross; in an Arabian prophet sitting in a cave and listening to divine revelations; in the playful Krishna charming female cow herders; in Buddha meditating under the Bodhi tree; in an aboriginal singer; and in a Celtic thin place. In fact, the lively omnipresent God makes every place a thin place, revealing holiness to those whose senses are acute.

A dynamic God inspires a sensational and creative spirituality. We can "taste and see" the beauty and goodness of God. We can hear all creation praising its Creator. We can feel holiness in a "God with skin." We can smell divinity wafting forth from a kitchen where a meal is lovingly prepared. With Rumi, we can discover "a thousand ways to kneel and kiss the ground." This same spirit is found in the Chinese aphorism, attributed to Mao Zedong, "Let a hundred flowers bloom; let a hundred schools of thought contend." Sadly, the Chairman's idealism was short-lived as the rage for order, power, and uniformity overwhelmed the seeds of diversity and creative transformation.

Today the joy of religious variety inspires us to explore new and creative forms of spirituality. Diversity is an opportunity for inclusion, innovation, and adventurous embracing of life's wondrous variety.

SPIRITUAL OPENINGS

Let us rejoice in the wondrous diversity of all creation. Let us celebrate the many pathways to God, whose loves embraces each and all of us. God has a personal relationship with each and every one of us, presenting us with unique possibilities for our time and place congruent with the well-being of our companions on this good Earth. Accordingly, while there are tried-and-true spiritual practices emerging from the wisdom of the great world religions, the inspiration of indigenous peoples, and the creativity of new religious movements, we are always invited to be conscious co-creators with God and the evolving universe by initiating our own healthy and unique spiritual practices.

In this last spiritual opening, the invitation is simply this: Find time for a mini-retreat of a few hours for creativity and reflection, inspired by the insight that your personal experience is essential to the wondrous diversity of life. Like the color purple, described by Alice Walker, you have a special gift to the universe. As you experience the Divine Creativity moving through your life, what "wild and crazy" spiritual practices can you imagine emerging from your own life experience?

Don't be modest. God loves creativity and encourages innovations. Like the parent of a young child, God says, "Surprise me!" After you've conceived a spiritual practice, try it out. What does it feel like? Does it enhance your relationship with the Divine Creativity of the universe? Does it draw you closer to others? Be playful in your adventurous spiritual practices. After all, Divine Wisdom (Sophia) is described as the Creator's playmate in bringing forth the universe.

Instead of singing spiritual chants in a traditional fashion, I often make up lively tunes, sometimes in the spirit of rock 'n' roll or gospel, as a playful spiritual discipline. Remember that all traditional spiritual practices were once novel and suspect, received with some surprise or disdain.

Another spiritual practice that can transform your life is "praying with your eyes open" as you go about your day. In this spiritual opening, simply let your senses be wide open as you pray. Pause and notice the wondrous colors, shapes, sounds, textures, and smells of everyday life. Take it all in prayerfully with every breath and send forth a blessing upon everything you experience. Let your sitting, walking, or running—even swimming and lounging—become an adventure in experiencing the wonders of life in all its variety, and in joining all creation in prayer and praise.

FOURTEEN

THE BLESSING WAY

*I will bless you and make your name great,
so that you will be a blessing....
In you all of the families of the Earth shall be blessed.*

from Genesis 12:2–3

*Blessed are the poor in spirit,
for theirs is the kingdom of heaven.
Blessed are those who mourn,
for they will be comforted.
Blessed are the meek,
for they will inherit the earth.
Blessed are those who hunger and thirst for righteousness,
for they will be filled.
Blessed are the merciful, for they will receive mercy.
Blessed are the pure in heart, for they will see God.
Blessed are the peacemakers,
for they will be called children of God.
Blessed are those who are persecuted for righteousness' sake,
for theirs is the kingdom of heaven.*

the Beatitudes, Matthew 5:3–10

In beauty may I walk.
All day long may I walk.
Through the returning seasons may I walk.
On the trail marked with pollen may I walk.
With grasshoppers about my feet may I walk.
With dew about my feet may I walk....
With beauty before me, may I walk.
With beauty behind me, may I walk.
With beauty above me, may I walk.
With beauty below me, may I walk.
With beauty all around me, may I walk.
In old age wandering on a trail of beauty, may I walk.
In old age wandering on a trail of beauty, may I walk.
It is finished in beauty.
is finished in beauty.

from the Navajo Blessing Way

Blessed are the interdependent, imaginative, and grateful, for they shall experience God. Spirituality is ultimately concerned with beauty and blessing. The movement of the universe is toward beauty. You can delight in the beauty of a grasshopper munching on a leaf, a toddler inventing a game, or the birth of a galaxy. Despite war, violence, and tragedy, there is, as Thomas Merton and Parker Palmer assert, "a hidden wholeness," luring all things with the vision of beauty that is inherent in their nature and our own.

When the author of Genesis says that humankind is created in the image of God, it was a proclamation that we reflect the beauty and wisdom of God. But not only humankind reflects the Divine Image: the continuity of life characteristic of the evolutionary process suggests that we are part of a lively universe that gives us life and the ability to embody blessing and beauty in our lives. We are part of a beautiful universe that inspires and undergirds our own experiences of beauty.

Mother Teresa asserted that her mission was to do something beautiful for God and that the quest for beauty—to bless and be blessed—is the heart of the spiritual journey. We move from beauty to beauty and blessing to blessing as we travel the pathways of wholeness. There is no wall of separation in the Way of Blessing between creature and Creator. God and the world dynamically interact in each moment and every event. God calls from within and from without, and we can respond to the divine currents moving through our lives, embodying this same divine holiness to greater or lesser degrees. Our love for our neighbors and the nonhuman world brings delight and beauty to God's experience. We love God best by loving God's ongoing creation in all its varied manifestations.

In the pathway of blessing, we discover that action and contemplation and ethics and spirituality complement one another in the lively interdependence of life. Our love for creation radiates across the universe and within God's experience, and then returns to us the energy and inspiration to become agents of beauty and blessing in the world.

Abraham and Sarah go on an adventurous journey and become participants in a blessing way that transforms the world. They are blessed to be a blessing and so are we. The energy of love that courses through us finds its fulfillment in flowing into the lives of others. This is the message of Jesus's picture of the vines and branches. When we are consciously connected to the vine, and when our hearts, minds, spirits, and bodies are aligned with God's dynamic vision, we experience great joy and bear fruit that nourishes others.

In fact, we will discover that there are no "others." Unique though each one is, we are also one in spirit and bound together by the energy of love. We become persons of stature, for whom the well-being of others is joined with our own well-being. We become "little Christs" and blessed bodhisattvas whose compassion heals the Earth.

We began our adventure with a spiritual teacher's counsel, "Why not become fire?" We conclude with the same affirmation: You are the light of the world. You are the fire of the Spirit. You are the illumination of divinity. Give light, give life, and give warmth. Be enlightened, and enlighten. Let your light shine, blessing the world and everyone you meet. It is fulfilled in beauty.

Become fire!

REFERENCES

1. Brian McLaren, *Why Did Jesus, Mohammed, and Buddha Cross the Road? Christian Identity in a Multi-Faith World* (Nashville: Jericho Books, 2012).
2. Diana Butler Bass, *Christianity after Religion: The End of the Church and the Birth of a New Spiritual Awakening* (New York: HarperOne, 2013) and Phyllis Tickle, *The Great Emergence: How Christianity Is Changing and Why* (Ada, MI: Baker Books, 2012).
3. Deepak Chopra, *Jesus: A Story of Enlightenment* (New York: Harper One, 2009) and Thich Nhat Hanh, *Living Buddha, Living Christ* (New York: Riverhead Books, 2007).
4. Pema Chodron, *The Places that Scare You: A Guide to Fearlessness in Difficult Times* (Boulder, CO: Shambala Classics, 2002), 22.
5. To hear Mary Oliver read this poem, go to http://www.youtube.com/watch?v=16CL6bKVbJQ.
6. Namo Amida Butsu, poetically rendered "I place my life [or take refuge] in the hands of Amida Buddha and his compassion"
7. http:/hubblesite.org/gallery/
8. http://www.youtube.com/playlist?list=PLE4b494fDBF7136631
9. http:/www.pbs.org/wgbh/nova/physics/fabric-of-cosmos.html
10. http://cell.com/cell_picture_show-immunology
11. Patricia Adams Farmer, *Embracing a Beautiful God* (Seattle, WA: Create Space, 2013).
12. Walter Wink, *The Powers That Be: Theology for a New Millennium* (New York: Harmony, 2010).
13. Brahdarankyaka Upanishad 1.3.28.
14. See Bruce Epperly, *Healing Marks* (Gonzales, FL: Energion Publications, 2013), *God's Touch: Faith, Wholeness, and the Healing Miracles of Jesus* (Louisville, KY: Westminster/John Knox, 2001), and *Healing Worship: Purpose and Practice* (Cleveland, IL: Pilgrim Press, 2006).
15. For more on artist-singer-songwriter Dawn Avery, see www.dawnavery.com
16. Agnes Sanford, *Healing Light* (New York: Ballantine Books, 1983), 14.
17. Ibid., 20.
18. Richard Rohr, *A Lever and a Place to Stand: The Contemplative Stance, the Active Prayer* (Mahwah, NJ: Hidden Spring, 2011), viii.
19. Susan Trout, *To See Differently* (Washington DC: Three Roses Press, 1990).
20. A more traditional rendition is "Be just, for it is closer to piety."
21. Walter Brueggeman, *Praying the Psalms: Engaging Scripture and the Life of the Spirit* (Eugene, OR: Wipf and Stock, 2007).
22. Rohr, 79–80.

23. "Tikkun HaKlali," translated by Rabbi Avraham Greenbaum, http://www.azamra.org/Esssential/general.htm
24. Thich Nhat Hanh, *Peace Is Every Step* (New York: Bantam, 1991), ix.
25. C. Austin Miles, "In the Garden" (1912).
26. Lauren Artress, *Walking a Sacred Path: Rediscovering the Labyrinth as a Spiritual Tool* (New York: Riverhead, 1995).
27. C. Austin Miles, "In the Garden" (1912).
28. Thich Nhat Hanh, *The Energy of Prayer: How to Deepen Your Spiritual Practice* (Berkeley, CA: Parallax Press, 2006), 122.

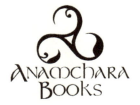

www.AnamcharaBooks.com

www.ingramcontent.com/pod-product-compliance
Lightning Source LLC
LaVergne TN
LVHW091531130125
801144LV00032B/315